STITCHES

Because Some Wounds Need More Than A Band-Aid Cure

Jeremy L. Blunt

Disclaimer: Upland Avenue Publishing Group and Jeremy L. Blunt make no representations or warranties with respect to the accuracy or completeness of the contents of this work and specifically disclaim all warranties, including without limitation warranties of fitness for a particular purpose. No warranty may be created or extended by sales or promotional materials. The advice and strategies contained herein may not be suitable for every situation. The work is sold with the understanding that the Publisher is not engaged in rendering legal, accounting, medical, therapy, or other professional services. The work is also sold with the understanding that the author is not engaged in rendering any kind of therapy or counseling services. If professional assistance is required, the services of a competent professional person should be sought.

Neither the Publisher nor the Author shall be liable for damages arising therefrom. The fact that a website or organization is referred to in this work as a citation and/or a potential source of further information does not mean that Upland Avenue Publishing Group or Jeremy L. Blunt endorses the information or organization or website.

STITCHES Because Some Wounds Need More Than A Band-Aid Cure
ISBN: 978-0-9960401-8-1
Library of Congress Control Number: 2015930531

©2015 by Upland Avenue Publishing Group. All rights reserved, including the right to reproduce this book, or portions thereof, in any form. No part of this publication may be used or reproduced, transmitted, downloaded, decompiled, reverse engineered, in any form or by any means, mechanical or electronic, including photocopying and recording, or by any information storage or retrieval system, without the permission in writing from Upland Avenue Publishing Group (except by a reviewer, who may quote brief passages and/or show brief video clips in a review). The scanning, uploading, and distribution of this book via the Internet or via any other means without the permission of the publisher is illegal and punishable by law.

Dedication

I would like to dedicate the reading and knowledge gained from the pages that follow to all who have impacted my journey and assisted in navigating my way.

To my wife, LaTrisha, my two daughters, Kaylie and Amerie, my parents, Elton and Barbara, my siblings, Terryln and Elnita and to my dearest friends and supporters who have supported me and encouraged me along the way, your words and expressions of care will always be held so dear to me. I love all of you dearly. Thank you for entertaining me and having patience as I continue to come into my own. I am who I am because of you. Thank you for allowing me to be a part of your lives.

Table of Contents

Introduction: So What Are Stitches Exactly?

Chapter 1: A Challenge for Change 1

Chapter 2: The Recipe 7

Chapter 3: Misconception of Love 17

Chapter 4: Ask the Man 26

Chapter 5: Communication is the Key 42

Chapter 6: It Starts with Self 51

Chapter 7: Learn Who You Are 57

Chapter 8: Is Love Alone Enough? 67

Chapter 9: Learn What You Want: Creating an Executable Plan 77

Chapter 10: A Realistic Vantage Point 81

Chapter 11: Baggage 88

Chapter 12: Get Over Them 96

Chapter 13: Trying is Not the Same as Giving It Your All 103

Chapter 14: Don't Quit Short 109

Chapter 15: Rain 119

Chapter 16: Why Do We Stay? 133

Chapter 17: Compromise vs. Negotiating 139

Chapter 18: When to Hold and When to Fold 145

Chapter 19: Change is Reflective 158

Chapter 20: Moving Forward 161

Chapter 21: Change in Perspective 166

Introduction

So What Are Stitches Exactly?

When a person endures an injury which fluids begin leaking or the outer layer of their skin has been breached, they require medical attention. They may require what medical professionals often refer to as surgical suture; more commonly known as "stitches". According to Webster's Dictionary, this is a procedure used to hold body tissues together after an injury or surgery. A few years ago I injured my foot exercising. When the injury first occurred, I conducted a series of home remedies. I looked online and found out I had symptoms of what I would later find to be true and that of plantar fasciitis. But nothing I did seem to truly solve the problem. The pain was excruciating so I finally went to see my doctor. My initial visits only resulted in him recommending routine recommendations. It was not until I had exhausted numerous other possible solutions that my doctor felt compiled to do a more aggressive treatment. In 2013, I had a surgical procedure on my left heel which required stitches. It was then that I began thinking about what the true purpose and need was for stitches. Although they hindered me from doing some things I was use to in my daily routine, they were necessary for my body to heal. The stitches did not leave me without scares but they allowed me to let my body matriculate through the natural healing process that was needed.

Understanding this I began to think about two things, one, what if I was impatient and did not get stitches or let the stitches do their job and two, how does this relate to how we relate to each other and our life experiences? What if I forced myself to use a quick fix instead of going through the steps I really needed? What if I just put a Band-Aid on the gaping wound on my heel? The normal response would be that by not giving myself proper or adequate attention, I would risk making my situation worst. This is true but this is what we do in relation to our lives every day. We go through life not wanting to be patient and allow the natural healing process to take place in our lives and only cause ourselves further damage. We figure we can stick a "Band-Aid" on the problem and keep trucking along. From the married couple who ignores issues in their relationship and figures they will heal themselves if they just don't talk about them, to the single person who has been with a series of partners but cannot seem to figure out why their relationships keep ending in the same result. I have heard and agree with the person who said that life is a classroom and our experiences are the teachers. Our problem comes when we choose to ignore the teachers and figure we can just coast thru the lessons without paying any attention to what is being instructed to us. Allow me to demonstrate with a mini story

A man was walking down the street and came upon a couple who appeared to be in the heat of a very intense discussion. From what the man could gather, the two were named Conventional and Out of the Ordinary. The issue lied in that Out of the Ordinary was trying to convey to Conventional that they were, in fact, on the same page. Conventional would not accept such a concept, he was so convinced that Out of the Ordinary was making up stuff and trying to make a mockery of his ways that he just did not want to give Out of the Ordinary a chance. After several moments of listening, the man finally interjected, "People, this is no way to live life. We all need each other. Conventional, you have to understand that the only thing that is constant is change and if you do not evolve with it, it will leave you behind. So stop complaining about it." And to Out of the Ordinary, he said, "Stop fighting Conventional; after all, it was he who was here first. You would not know what it means to be different if you did not have something to base it off of." We all want to have our own identity but it cannot come at the expense of forsaking those who made it possible. Learn from

Conventional so you cannot just be known as Out of the Ordinary but Extraordinary.

This book is about recognizing the lessons of life and learning to use those lessons as "Stitches" to help guide us through future life experiences. The greatest tragedy is to go through lessons and not use them for future experiences. I am not a relationship or life guru. I do believe I have been blessed with a unique gift of showing others things that were right in front of their faces or along their paths all along but they were either too caught up in witnessing life's experiences that the lessons have waved with empty responses as they passed by. This is what "STITCHES" are all about because honestly, some wounds need more than a Band-aid cure. There has been enough covering up wounds with quick bandages when it requires a more aggressive treatment and stitches to ensure that the recovery is done right.

Chapter 1:

A Challenge for Change

One day I was sitting and recalling the happenings of the day, I often replay the events that occurred and how I handled them but this day I was compelled to challenge myself. Two thoughts rage through my mind: 1) what are we doing about the less fortunate and 2) what are we doing to help the uninformed? Earlier that day I was riding in downtown Baton Rouge and although I first thought I had taken a wrong turn, I was soon reminded that what often appears to be a wrong turn for us is in fact the right turn for an appointed event. As I turned down a street, to get back to where I was supposed to be, I noticed three people standing on the side of the road. They were standing on a corner. One lady, talking on her cell phone, appeared to be in a stressful state. As I drove closer, I noticed a gentleman standing next to what looked to be a disfigured bike. Then, I saw a man lying on the pavement. He appeared to be almost lifeless. My initial instinct was to stop and offer my assistance but I realized the cargo I was transporting was time sensitive and I was already cutting it close. As I slowed down, four to five more people appeared from nowhere but still there was no movement from the man. While they all were probably concerned, no one ventured over to the man on the ground. I wondered and pondered of ways that I could be of assistance, but my mind drew blanks. I reluctantly convinced myself that the situation was being handled by the other people on the scene and that the emergency personnel would soon arrive. With that, I proceeded on with my day and my task. As I moved further down the street, I intensely looked and listened for speeding emergency vehicles and piercing sirens but there was nothing. Once I completed my delivery, there was a passing thought to go back and check on the victim. This thought quickly became a fleeting notion once I glanced at my watch and recalled the next item on my agenda. Morning transitioned into afternoon which progressed into evening and with every moment that my mind rested, I was haunted by the unfolding of the day. I became fixated on the concept of change and all that must occur for change to actually happen. I thought about my part in the small incident that although I did not lay witness to, I was present for the aftermath. I found myself quoting the famous slogan from Spider Man which states, "With great power comes great responsibility." As I sit and think these things over, I wonder why people claim to want change but are not willing to do what is necessary to see the change manifest. It takes more than a desire or a want. It takes a personal get up and do it to see change happen.

We wake each morning with a personal agenda for the day. The guy did not know he would be struck lifeless by a car at a quarter 'til one. None of those who passed by expected to lay witness to a death scene. I did not know that my wrong turn would take me right to a pivotal position to make a difference. The sad irony of all this is that every day we see people who are physically, mentally and spiritually lifeless. We watch them and know they are headed for destruction. We waste a lot of time placing the blame and shifting the responsibility. Sometimes we slow down just enough to be nosey and see what is happening, but we quickly detach and conclude that because we are not directed connected, we are not in any way effected.

At that moment, I challenge myself with question after question. What could I have done? What do I need to do to get others off the sidelines and involved? How many more young people are we going to let ruin their lives because we did not feel like dealing with them? Does it really matter if they respond negatively toward us? Are we not mature enough to look past their immaturity?

Life is Coming. Rushing It Just Adds Unnecessary Stress

One of our biggest shortfalls, as humans, is we want everything at the snap of a finger or the blink of an eye. Judging by most, yesterday was too late. We have very little to no patience. What is worse is that we seldom have a clue as to what we really want- we only think we do. Anyone over age thirty will tell you most of the decisions they made and things they thought they wanted when they started out are not what they think and often what they want now. I can recall saying some things and believing some things and now… those things are but a thing of the past. Some of my earliest memories are filled with a desire to be older, to want to drive, to have a girlfriend and to do adult stuff. Like so many others, I pressed toward that mark despite often times making it harder for myself. And if that isn't enough, we often involve others in our mayhem.

For as long as I can remember I have been one that people come to talk to about their problems. When it first started I do not remember ever inviting anyone to, I was just always perceived as being older. Often it results in me giving some wisdom that even baffles me sometimes. I had the opportunity to speak with a couple who admitted to having a few problems. They both agreed that individual work was needed to improve their relationship. Shortly afterwards, they decided to break up.

As one of their biggest fans, I do understand that every relationship must run its course and it is not always easy. After one party expressed the need to separate, I was still convinced they could very well end up back together. In many relationships, people fail to notice the individual problems they have and the need to work them out individually. A couple is defined as two individuals of the same sort considered to be together by marriage, engagement, or otherwise closely associated. Because they are made up of two individuals, they come with individual issues that oftentimes existed before they got together. In the medical world they would call these preexisting conditions. Some issues can be resolved as a couple, while others require separation. Knowing the difference between the two is essential.

Several months later, the couple was back together and attempting to work things out. They called and requested assistance on the journey but our schedules never coincided. Time passed and we lost touch for a season. All of a sudden I received an unexpected visit from the couple who were proud to say they had gotten married. Although I was taken by surprise, I desired nothing but happiness for them. The genuine smiles on their faces were the obvious indications that they were happy together. They went on to explain why I was not kept informed of their progress and how they felt the need to immediately "jump the broom". Despite my urging for them to seek counseling when

I found out that they had not, they assured me that they would work things out on their own and it would be fine. Needless to say, the marriage lasted six months before they were back at each other's throat, claiming they had made the biggest mistake of their lives. When they finally came to see me, I asked why they seem to be reluctant and what took them so long. They told me they did not want to hear the age old "I told you so". This is the reason why so many people don't get the help they need when they need it. Please do not put off matters because you do not want to admit that they are serious. It has been proven statistically that the earlier you deal with your problems, and often this means going to see someone, the increased probability you have in successfully working out your problems.

Do not be like this couple, so concerned about the response of other people that they did not realize if they had just made a few changes in their actions, things could have turned out extremely different. *STITCHES#108 - Life is not a race. It's coming. Stop rushing.* Starting before we know ourselves we begin to develop the notions of what we want out of a relationship, marriage, school, job, and life. From there we forge forward to make those thought processes a reality. Yes, I am talking about dreams. I am also not saying they are wrong. We all need them in order to have something to work toward. *STITCHES #87 - The problem most people have with dreams is not navigating to them.*

Chapter 2

The Recipe

Are you evolving or are you suffering from the side effects of things changing around you? This question did not make sense to me six to eight months ago; partially because I have been forced to evolve even during the course of writing this book. I came into the writing of this book with one perspective and although I felt other people were entitled to their opinions, I felt strongly enough in my own that I was not going to allow my perspective to be obscured or tainted in any way. This was, however, until I started talking to people and really listening- instead of just hearing them. In order to paint the total picture, take a look at my original vantage point. Your feelings are valid. I simply ask that you open your eyes to see the full picture in relation to the one that has been guided by your upbringing.

Here was my first concept...

It started as far back as you can remember. At first it was like an unthinkable disgust. Then in what felt like an overnight transition, we saw our world in a whole new light. There was a time when we would turn the television station from one of our favorite shows as soon as something "mushy" started happening. We watched and sometimes participated in grade-school mockery of those who may have contracted the age old "cooties". Only to find ourselves years down the road dedicating what can merely be described as a large part of our lives to either finding that one special person in the world to share our "cooties" or goodies with or sharing it with as many people as we can while simultaneously experiencing there's. So what then made the difference for us? How do we know that what we have been experiencing has not been one of humanity's greatest mistakes?

When you ask most people to describe what they view as the meaning of love, they will give you an array of descriptions. Due to life experiences, their definitions are more often than not slanted. I surveyed a variety of people as I was writing this book and although I will not disclose any names of particulars, I did find the information very informative. I also found striking resemblance in responses to say that none of those surveyed could see each other's responses. When it came to the subject of love, most people describe love as a noun; the giving of one's own mind, body, and soul or the commitment of one to another physically, mentally, emotionally, and physical. How they feel about others or how they are made to feel. Everyone has their own definition of love. This is because we have been wired to think of love as a noun. A noun of course by definition is a person, place, or thing. But when asked how you would describe love, more than likely you would use other words that in themselves are nouns- not the specific word 'love.' Do not be alarmed. It is not your fault. We think of love as certain things that occur as a result of being in love. We call it love when someone is honest, committed, and respectful. The truth about the word "love" is that it is but an emotion and a feeling. Therefore, love is a verb. A verb, by definition, is a word used to describe an action, state, or occurrence. We take the sum total of events that transpire and conclude that IT MUST BE LOVE.

This is how the fantasy began. Before we even knew what love was, we saw our parents sharing a moment of intimacy; we saw a glimpse of two people staring in each other's eyes on television and something just clicked in our minds. It told us that whatever this was, everyone seemed to be searching for "it". "It", whatever it is, is definitely something worth looking into or trying for ourselves.

Being that we thirst after knowledge and recognizing that we are a constantly evolving human species, we concluded quickly that something is wrong with a large portion of the population's formula because they cannot seem to get "it" right. At first it was just one or two couples who after having relationship problems, could not work through their issues so they went their separate ways. It was hardly ever discussed and even when it was it was all hear say. Gradually, this percentage of failed traditional relationships increased to half of the number of relationships and or marriages ending in divorce. Now, failure is so common that people create an exit strategy before creating goals for their relationship. These new statistics caused people to start analyzing and critiquing what was going wrong with relationships and ultimately the design of them.

I grew up in the South and anyone from there can tell you about one of its most prized cuisines- GUMBO. Gumbo is like a stew or thick soup. It got its origin from the Creole people in some of the southernmost parts of Louisiana in the early 1800s. The thick mixture starts with what is called a roux and additional ingredients are added such as chicken, poultry, seasoning, greens, and okra. Any Southerner who is familiar with this delicacy will tell you, the key to a good gumbo is not just knowing and adding all the ingredients but possessing the ability to taste and see, smell, and adjust accordingly to make sure the gumbo results is a delectable delight. This brings us to the point of analyzing the high failure rate when the formula is so simple.

The analysis has resulted into people looking for alternative means to find relationship happiness or satisfaction. The most common alternative is a belief that the formula that makes up the key ingredients must be faulty. Others choose to either do nothing or use the exact same recipe or attempt not to use the recipe at all. People try the same recipe others have used with hopes for success, recomposing the formula, or choosing not participate.

Using the Same Ole Formula

Albert Einstein defined insanity as doing the same thing over and over again, expecting different results. I believe this is what a person does if they just look at someone else's recipe for a successful relationship and figure they will do the same thing and get the same results. This is the reason why there are so many heartbroken daughters who are looking for a husband based on their parents' relationship. I do believe at one time in history this formula was able to be replicated, and it worked successfully- but not in this century. With the introduction of technology and the evolution of society, this has left many a victim of negative consequences as in a game of Russian Roulette.

Recomposed Formula

There are the various versions to a recomposed formula. With all formulas, however, there are side effects; some good, others not so much. One formula derived from watching Fathers fail and simply take up space. This along with the advancement of women's rights resulted in women standing up. Women began to express to men how they felt. They confronted their concerns with the way some men stopped taking care of their responsibilities as the head of the house. The negative side effect is that fathers were embarrassed and took further steps back. The result: An epidemic of fatherless homes. The positive is that women have stepped up and proven they can still get the job done.

Not taking anything away from women but every home needs both parents to be present and doing their part. It is like building a house and one day having the electrician decide they are not going to do their part for whatever reason. The contractor can say to themselves they have been around enough electricians that they are not going to contract out for another one. They could choose to do it themselves with the thought that they would save themselves some hassle and headache. At the end of the day, they would essentially save in some retrospect but at what cost? An experienced electrician pays for himself in the long run.

Trying to fill in for someone who is designed for the job is a big risk with long term consequences. We cannot make a father who has chosen not to do their part in their child's life but there are enough "father figures" out there that if approached correctly will gladly "contract in."

Another recomposed formula is the type of partner. The original formula is that of a man and a woman. This is where the man is the leader in the family; the provider and the woman is the helper to her husband. Helper does not mean less equal. Many have found flaw in this formula so in their calculations, they believe the answers to making a success story may lie in this aspect of the original formula being wrong. They search for a partner who is like them but different. The thought process and their desire is to find someone with the same qualities that the opposite sexual orientation was born with but without the risk of unfamiliarity. Why go through the process of teaching the opposite sex and having them learn you when you can just find someone who is already similar to you in sex and just familiarize them to what you desire? In a way, just take short cuts to get to the perfect person.

When asked how many people believed there was such a thing as a perfect person, an overwhelming number said they believed there was no such thing. If the quest is to find happiness, where did the belief come from that just because you have not found your "soul mate" that it is ok to go out and find someone else who has not found theirs either and consciously proceed to re-orchestrate the process?

If this is the formula you have chosen to use, please do not misunderstand me, my only question is how do you define your love and happiness? Love and happiness should not come at the cost of spending the majority of your time defending your love and happiness. It is not about belief or religion because if that were the case, then you would have run from this lifestyle a long time ago. The second question about this chosen formula is do you do it purely to show your pride in your ability to make a decision? Research has shown that homosexual relationships are tremendously less likely to be successful than heterosexual ones. In The Sexual Organization of the City, University of Chicago Sociologist Edward Laumann argues that "typical gay city inhabitants spend most of their adult lives in 'transactional' relationships, or short-term commitments of less than six months."[1]. The point is to test the validity of the real purpose of this formula. Have the results proven to be less successful than that of a heterosexual lifestyle. Don't be offended that I'm questioning your chosen lifestyle. I did not say you were wrong. This is simply a conclusion which can be derived once a belief is incorporated into the equation. I believe that those who choose the homosexual lifestyles should be afforded the same rights as those living in other lifestyles. However, there should be different titles. Just because a person chooses to live a certain way does not mean that they are less than human. As such, their right to live, be, and love whomever they choose is their option. Too many times we pawn off our beliefs and opinions on people who did not ask for them in the first place. Everyone is seeking to be happy. How a person chooses to do this or their path to get there is, honestly, nobody's business but there's. My goal is to just ask you to examine relationships with me along with everyone else who reads this and decide if the path you have chosen or are choosing is the best for the results you find acceptable.

The next recomposed formula is lifelong singleness. People typically choose this lifestyle out of desperation and frustration. To others, it is because they are "sooooo" tired of the poor relationships they have found themselves in. The truth is the problem is they did not want to take enough alone time before anyone else came along to learn themselves and therefore they had very little to nothing to offer and constantly fell victim to wolves in sheep's clothing came along. As a result, they failed miserably and was left life shambled once again. This is a public service announcement - **some things we bring on ourselves so stop blaming others**. A dog is a dog. You can bath it, sweet talk it, and dress it all up but unless you recognize what it is, realize its limitations and treat it based on these first two, you are fighting a lost cause. Bottom line, you cannot blame the dog for being a dog if that is all the dog has ever known. You must make the adjustments on your end based on what you have. Learn to be by yourself and learn who and what you want. I often tell people like this, *STICHES #2 - You have to know what makes you tick before you can teach anyone else how you tick or how to not tick you off.* The problem remains because the recipe we have been hoping would give us different results have still been based on using the same "rule." Until you cure the main ingredient, nothing will come out the way you ultimately desire.

Chapter 3

Misconception of Love

Have you ever taken the time to think why you do some of the things you do? Why do you befriend the people that you do? Why do some people remain close to their family while others dart for the exit as soon as it becomes available? These are all questions that should be examined and explored by everyone. To learn who you are, you must take some time to figure out your thought pattern. Most people just tarry on through life from one experience to the next. When one goes "south", they just look for another ride. I called this is a gambler's mentality. I believe this mentality just plays and prays for luck. Some things should not be left to chance; especially in the case of love.

Love is but an experience. Yes, it is described by many different things but more than any other it is an experience. Just like any other experience in our lives, we choose what to keep in the forefront of our memory bank. When it comes to love we mostly think of the extreme highs and the most dreadful lows. When you ask most people about their love experiences they will tell you about the sweetest moments. Like their first date or the sweetest thing someone has ever done for them. Men might say it was the woman that made him pause from looking at any other. And then there is the other end of the spectrum. You have the dreadful lows that people will sing their sob stories about- how they were abused, taken for granted, and just misused; even the regrets and the ones that got away. Don't get me wrong. I'm not trying to discredit these moments but the keys to success in love actually lie in the neutrality of these times. It is thought be a naturally human behavior to reside in this thought process and in the moments that make memories but this behavior is actually learned. We get our thought processes on how love should operate by watching other people's moments. For instance, one of the most entertaining types of shows on the market today are reality shows. So many people are glued to the television to witness other people's most memorable moments. I'm not just talking about the Housewives of XYZ but also shows like American Idol and Biggest Loser. We really do not want to see the process but rather the product. To entertain us, we are kept on our heels and involved by asking us to vote and be a part of the show sometimes; when all the while, the results have already been predetermined. We have become a society interested only in results. It's not really important to us how they get there but we want to know what happens if they fail and what it is like if they succeed. If you are disagreeing, ask yourself, when was the last time you kept up with an artist who was let go off of one of the shows? Have you ever written a contestant once they finish the show? We have become a result driven society and it is this mindset which has driven our love lives out of sync.

When it comes to love we should be looking at all facets of our lives. When we are involved with someone, we should look at the regular every day experiences; the day to day activities. There is where you will find the answers to your love questions. Look past the initial sparks and stars. I'm talking about after the wanting to stay up and talk on the phone all night and the playfulness of who will hang up first. You have to wait until both of you are at your norms with each other. Unfortunately so many people see this phase as the launching pad of their love and jump right into a substantially permanent situation. The initial butterfly feelings and anxiousness are but steps to the foundation. Love is so complicated at times that these steps are necessary in order to build a stage for everything else that will take place. Look at the relationship as a concert about to unfold. You know it is coming so there are certain things that must happen in order to get ready for it. A stage has to be set up. The beginning parts of setting up the stage are the steps and the risers. I do not know anyone who would get completely carried way with just seeing risers in place. They would be excited because they know the preparation has begun but they would not go to the concert sight and pitch camp yet. They would at least wait until the floor of the stage is in place. Do not get so caught up with the show that you are there too early in anticipation and you become exhausted before the show ever gets started.

Take in these parts of the preamble of the relationship so you can see the potential of your partner. Stop expecting the feelings that you and your partner have at the beginning to last forever. They don't. The initial spark will fade. The key is replacing this "initial magic" with something tangible. Not replacing this can result in a relationship deteriorating. It will begin the moment the initial magic fades. For some, this process will take years before you could even realize something is missing. In other relationships, you may know almost in an instant. I am not talking about replacing it with a child or children because this will only postpone the inevitable. This is the reason why people get divorced after being married twenty or so years. They claim they stick or stuck it out for the sake of the offspring but the truth is that they were lazy. Al Duncan, a good friend of mine and a nationally renowned motivational speaker, often tells people that life is filled with choices and in making those choices you can either do what is right or what is easy. The reason so many people suck at relationships is that they have chosen to go with what seemed easy so many times they cannot distinguish that which is right anymore. *STITCH #98 - Know your weapons as well as your fight and make smarter choices.* I am talking about creating something more tangible than just beginning with a friendship. Although this is important, we are talking about creating something that is deeper than friendship. After all, we all have had friends we grew up with and then just drifted apart from. It made you even wonder if you were really as good of friends as you first thought anyway.

REPLACE MAGIC WITH JOY

Magic is only a temporary state of happiness. Some would say happiness and joy is the same thing but I beg to differ. Happiness is dependent upon circumstances and situations. It is based on your state of being at the time. It is what brought you to that point and what sustains you during that period. Joy, on the other hand, is an ongoing process regardless of what is going on and whether you can do anything about it. Joy is the basic element of being. This is not something you develop once you meet someone but is what you have already. It is what you bring into the relationship. Each person must have joy for themselves. Joy is the feeling of life's experiences. It is the evolutionary spectacle of change.

One of the most dangerous things we face is the very thing as a human we hold in the highest regard, free will. With this great honor lies also a twin-horror. The freedom to will allows us to see potential as opportunity. I believe the opposite of this opportunity is the concept of options. For biblical scholars, in the beginning of time there was a tree that man was ordered to and forbidden to eat from and it was called the tree of the knowledge of good and evil. Man, as the story is told, ate from it. Although he did not die a physical death, it altered history and his relationship with his creator. The tree changed man's vision from seeing the opportunity in things to seeing all the options available. Options are dangerous in the hands of anyone not mature enough to see the consequences of actions. They are dangerous because when we begin to view areas of our lives as options, it changes our perspective and how we proceed. Anyone who has been through a relationship can testify of when they first decided it was time to move on. If they were in a committed relationship or marriage this was not an open shut decision that was just decided and acted upon overnight. It took time and planning. This all came after the concept of options. Many times we cripple our own decisions because we view them as options. When we are married to someone, divorce should not be an option. However, so many marriages play the cards of their life and relationship with divorce being the joker or secret weapon. They play this card whenever they feel the time is most conducive for them. Divorce should not be an option. It should be one of the cards at the bottom of the deck after you have played all your possibilities. In life we face many challenges. Let me also take a moment to say that I do understand that there are times when you have to go straight to the bottom of the deck. This is not as a result of an option but in rare or few cases where plays that are made are so abrupt they force you to react out of desperation or for the sake of life itself. It also needs to be said that options in the hands of anyone, at any age, which is not mature enough to handle them or make wise decisions, can lead to a state of destruction; both for them and all others involved. It is the perspective by which we view those challenges which ultimately determine the outcome. The ability to see ourselves in a position is our greatest weapon. We have a tendency to believe what we hear and act it out even if it is done subconsciously. An example of this is when you hear people speak of the power one has in their tongue and how after saying or listening to someone's problem or predict a certain outcome, the results can greatly influence the end results. Have you ever been around someone who said they get sick around this time every year and they actually do shortly thereafter? You have to understand the power of influence you have over your own life. If you want a better marriage, start talking positively about it. If you want a better relationship with your in-laws or your supervisor at work, start talking and acting like the situation is better then what it looks like. *STICHES #96 We must become the change we want to see.*

When most people think of change, they think of not wanting to stop doing what they are doing. They think of how people are asking them to change what they believe. Even if it is not fine, they are still reluctant to want that type of change. This is because true change comes from within. If it is forced by an outside influence, it is not really the change desired but the force that accompanies. Let's try viewing change as watching a person walk down the street in one direction and then being asked to change because others feel as though they are headed the wrong way. The first issue here is that it is an outside influence causing an uncomfortable feeling to occur and hence cause the person to change. Because it was by an outside influence, the person may turn with the impression that nothing that they were doing was right and they needed to turn abruptly one hundred and eighty degrees in the opposite direction. The problem with this is that if you can visualize that person walking down the street and abruptly turning one hundred and eighty degrees in the completely opposite direction, then their progress has been stunted. It seems like they are going right back down the path from which they came but since it is impossible to repeat the same thing their path is actually different. The manifestation of that change may just have not occurred yet. To top this off, other changes may occur and cause another abrupt change. We have already discussed side affects but it is worth repeating. There is an old saying that you can take a horse to water but you cannot make it drink. This is true but yet we attempt to every time we try and force change down someone else's throat. We must learn to just guide them to place of change and allow the light bulb to come on in its own time. This is called personal change. Personal change is when a person draws the conclusion that things need to be changed in their life. This is not based on other's influence but rather on self-observation and self-evaluation. I met this aspiring young lady and I remember jokingly mentioning in our talk that the key to establishing real change in others is getting them to turn their light bulb on. It sounds easy but I assure you it is far from it. Like the old saying goes, "you can take a horse to the water but you cannot make it drink." This is one of life's biggest challenges. If I could bottle up the ingredients to make the light bulbs in other's head come on, possibilities would be endless. The truth is that we cannot turn the light bulb on no more than we can make the horse drink. This is the only change that is true to that person although it may or may not be permanent. It is the only change whereby a person is whole heartedly into their decision. When a person changes based on other people's opinions or influence, they never really give the new direction their all. It is like watching a person come back down the street but yet constantly looking around and behind in obvious uncertainty. Sooner or later disaster will be waiting because just as you cannot serve two masters, you cannot go two different directions at the same time.

Chapter 4

Ask the Man

I used to write for a Magazine and they had a section entitled "Ask the Man". The words from those who wrote in looking for answers were very real. They faced real problems and needed real solutions. I often get asked questions about particular situations and I felt this could help someone who may be reading this so I have included a few.

Dear Ask the Man,

I am saved and desperate and what I mean by that is I believe in Prayer in the Word of God first above all things. I have been married for eight years to a man who I know can be Loving, Caring, Kind, and Definitely a Man of God! That was the man I married. Nothing in the world mattered more to him. Know your weapons as well as your fight and make smarter choices than God, Himself, Me, and our Twins; at least that's what I thought. When we met and before we got married he knew I was sick. I told him about my disease and so did the Pastor before we got married. Before I fast forward I have an inherited blood disorder that is very painful and there is no cure. While we were dating he used to come to the hospital every day before class and before work. He never missed a day whenever I would go in. He used to care! We have been through many difficult times together struggling with the birth of our twins, the loss of his parents and grandparents, and the diagnosis of me having Breast Cancer and a repeat within six months. So yes, we have been through a lot. We were young and in Love. Nothing else in the world mattered. We were happy to be just in each other's presence! He was the perfect gentlemen and I was head over hills in love. We Loved God and Our Lil Family- just the four of us. The first place we went together was to Church. When he asked me to go he was in total shock that I said, "Yes!" He was truly Heaven Sent! Now here comes the storm...the devil called "ADULTERY!" My husband has been cheating for several years now. It really got bad after the cancer. He started taking our boys with him to females' houses when I was either in the ER or in the hospital. He would stop for a while and then start again. Whenever I said I was leaving he would change only for a little while. I would ask to go to therapy and when I would set it up we would never go. I have been to several different churches because we move a lot (military life) and I have talked to several different pastors. I have been praying and I'm still praying. My boys tell me I should leave because their daddy cheats on me a lot. They can tell me his game up and down from the type of women he talks to the ones he avoids. He tells them not to get married until they are 40 or older and then he asks them if the women are fine that he talks to. He tells these women that he's not married, he has the boys and he doesn't know where I am. From city to city and state to state there are many different women. I have read text messages where he says he is not married and doesn't have any kids. There is some talk about the females going down on him and them asking for the favor in return. I have talked to several different women who have been brainwashed and lied to by my husband- from strippers, to college students to teens at the age of 18-20. He has messed with females in the same apartment complex or on the same street as us. They have all been close to where we lived. Never far at all; I mean Right under My Nose. I have had women crying on the phone because they had fallen for his lies. He would take money out the bank to wine and dine them while he chewed me out if I spent $5.00. He yells at our kids and says they are aggravating. He hits them for no reason at times and doesn't want to be bothered with them. That's his blood. He will take out time with other people's kids faster than his own. He has told me some harsh words over the last few years. He says stuff like I'm aggravating and annoying. He has no sympathy for me, doesn't care about me being sick and tells me to shut the fuck up whenever I'm in the hospital crying because of my pain. He would take family members (his cousins) with him to other females' houses also. He has messed with strippers and all! He just didn't care. Now he is sleeping on the sofa and the kids are sleeping with me. I didn't put him there. He put himself on the sofa. He would leave from work sometimes and not call or come 'til 2 am or even 5am sometimes. He no longer comes with us to church. He sometimes sneaked out the house. If I go and have a ladies night out, he drops the boys to my mom at about 11 pm and goes out without me knowing. He pretends to come and meet me then he hurries back home to make it seem like he's been there all night. Now know that when I did the chemo for the cancer it caused me to lose my sex drive at a young age and some meds sent my body through menopause super early. I was only 27! So we weren't having sex like we used to. He wanted to but I didn't have the urge to. I even tried taking meds to increase my sex drive. Did I drive him to those other women? Is he tired of me? Tired of being with me and me being sick? We don't even talk and when we do, we usually argue. I am trying. I even bought a flick and he told me to take it back because it was a sin. Seriously? I tried to change my sex habits or style and he ignores that. One night I finally told him I had enough. He called me crying and saying He can't live without me and that he would be lost without me! He needs me in his life and He wanted us to work. He said he would go to a marriage counselor because he wants his family. Can you please help? Give me some advice! Is it me? Is it because I'm sick? What Gives? Does he really love us?

Signed,

Saved & Desperate

Dear Saved & Desperate,

Thank you for sharing your thoughts and feelings during such a heart wrenching time in your life. I would like to start by reminding you that all things work together for the good of those that love God and who are called according to his purpose (*New International Version*, Romans 28:8). I reference this to let you know that this too shall pass. It may seem like you cannot see the light at the end of the tunnel but be encouraged that although you may not understand when you are going through it, know that the Father promised to give you the strength to get to the other side. With this being said, please allow me to give you some good hard advice. Let me begin by telling you that some people allow their faith to supersede their God-given common sense. Please do not be one of those people.

Most people get caught up on the concept of love and never take the time to understand love. Love is patient and kind. Love is patient, love is kind. It does not envy, it does not boast, it is not proud. (*New International Version*, 1 Cor. 13:4 & 7). The man who you fell in love with is in your past. I'm not saying that he does not still love you but because he does not understand love, he has lost how to allow the love in his heart to guide him. He goes from woman to woman trying to fill a void that God intended for you alone to fill. When a person makes a choice to marry someone and asks God to bless it, they are asking God to put a place holder in their heart that can only be filled by the one they are coming into covenant with. So many marriages fail because partners do not understand this and when things do not go as envisioned, they look for someone else to fill the vacancy. In your letter you speak of desperation. Desperation can be a dangerous thing if not channeled correctly. Before we address what your husband needs to do, you need to ask yourself if you have given up and if not are you willing to weather the storm to reclaim your marriage? Many times people have been hurt so badly by others to the point that they are not willing to try and recover. They waste their time trying to revive something they have in their own heart given up on. You need to search your heart and be sure of what you want moving forward. All too often we think we know what we are getting into only to find out that we do not know ourselves as well as we may have thought. Listen to me really well on the next sentence. YOUR SICKNESS IS NOT YOUR FAULT. Neither are the actions of your husband. There is a story in the bible where Jesus and his disciples came across a man who had been blind since birth and the disciples asked Jesus if it was something the blind man or his parents had done to cause him to be this way. Jesus' response to them was no, these things had happened in order to bring glory to God. I know you are writing expecting me to tell you whether it is okay for you to leave your husband. That is not my decision to make but yours. I would only advise that you come to your decision after prayer, deep thought, and after you have exhausted ALL options. An unknown author once said 'adversity does not build character, it reveals it.'

Many times we think we know someone but we really do not know them until we see them operating in times of test and trial. Once a person reveals who they truly are, we are to address that person, not the one we want to see. Stress does not help your situation so it is time to address the stressful things in your life that you can control. You need to identify the stressful factors and determine how you plan to resolve them. Everyone deserves to be happy.

Happiness is not something that comes only when things are perfect but when efforts are being made to make the best out of things. You need to have a conversation with your husband to address a couple of issues. #1 – The lack of honor he gives you as his wife. I get that he has lost hope and no longer feels he can handle the challenges of being with you but that does not give him permission to break his vows. There is no excuse for this and he will have to answer for them. The lies must stop. The disrespect in how he talks to you must end immediately. Very seldom do I recommend people to give their spouses an ultimatum, but your case is one of my exceptions. He either needs to honor his vows and commitment or divorce you and go on about his business. If he chooses to stay, he needs to schedule the counseling sessions and place parameters on himself. Those parameters need to be documented and verbally agreed on by you. This is not the time for you to just bark out orders but for clear and concise decisions to be made moving forward. I cannot stress how critical this is because it is the foundation for beginning again. He has to rebuild trust and he doesn't get credit for time already served. # 2 – The disrespect to the concept of family. If he gets past number one, this is the second thing he needs to address and fix. You are a family. He cannot substitute a less than desired sex life with random people.

Part of his vows were for better or worse until death do you part. You both must be willing to explore new things and do not think the other person is content with just giving up and not trying anymore. Sex is a factor in all relationships but only through communication can you determine to what degree. # 3 - The failure to be an honorable man to your children. Boys learn how to be men by watching other men. Your sons have been watching him. Although your sons are constantly telling you to leave him because of his cheating, they are being brainwashed into how to treat females. Unless corrected, they will eventually have commitment issues as well. It is a learned behavior. He needs to understand his role and use his mistakes as teaching tools. His sons need to see him honoring you. Your husband needs to understand that if he truly wants to amend things, he must be patient. The walls of Jericho weren't built in one day nor were they rebuilt in one day. He cannot expect everyone to be over his ills after a simple apology. It may take years to rebuild what was lost. If he is not truly in it for the long haul, he might as well not start. Otherwise, quitting cannot be an option.

None of us fully understand the gravity of the hands that we are dealt but we must play them to the best of our abilities based on the knowledge we have gained through experiences and beliefs. Too often we stay in situations and allow people to treat us wrongly based on how they were before the storms of life came. We all want picnics in the park on bright and sunny days but few realize that it is because of the stormy times that we hold those sunny days so dear. Love is a choice. We make it every day. Love is also an adjective. It is expressed by your time, how you talk to each other, what you do for one another, and so on. It is what you make of it. You can either choose to reinvest in what you have already established or just like in cards, you can throw in your hand and hope for a better deal. It is not guaranteed and you could end up with a much worse situation.

Lastly, I want to encourage you to keep your hands in God's hand regardless of how things manifest. Your faith may be tested but do not allow it to fail. There are still blessings in store for you. They might not be in the shape or form that we want but we have to trust that the Creator of the world has our best interest in mind. All is not lost and you should not count your marriage done until all options have been explored, however, be willing to move on if God sees fit. Everything happens for a reason and although we may not know why, the testimonies are worth the test.

Dear Ask the Man,

Let's call me, Rejection.

I have been depressed because every man who I think has an interest in me does not. They only want to see how much of my time and my money I can throw at them. I am 40 years old and had my share of poor choices. I am not a bad looking woman nor do I find myself overweight. Men lately have been a revolving door. Now don't get me wrong, I am not a promiscuous woman at all. I don't believe at my age and at the point in my life that I should be sleeping around. Ask the man I feel now and he'll say I will always be alone and never will have anyone who is genuine in my life to love me for me. I'm at the verge of giving up on this word called, "love" and live between the two walls I built for myself.

Dear Ask the Man Writer,

Thank you for writing and sharing your story with us. After reading your letter, a couple things were alarming. I understand that you have had your share of bad relationships or one night flings but don't be so quick to throw in the towel on love. With a few adjustments I believe you will find a renewed hope.

The first line of your letter indicates that there are some individual issues that need to be addressed first and foremost. It appears that you do not seem happy with yourself. Your specific description as to how you do not look exhibits that you are not satisfied with your outward appearance. This lack of self esteem has led to a sense or need to overcompensate for things you don't see in yourself. You find yourself feeling like you need to add to what you do for guys just to keep and maintain their attention.

The truth is, before you can find happiness from anyone else you must find it within. You must be able to look yourself in the mirror and be proud of what you see. Not only do you need to know who you are but also love yourself before you can teach someone else to love you. Your age is not a factor when it comes to love. Until you know what you want and stop settling for less than what you deserve or desire, you will continue to be disappointed. Additionally, all humans, not just men or women, will get away with whatever they're allowed to get away with. The men who seem to take advantage of you do it because you allow it and do not expect or demand more for yourself. As long as you give them money, they will take it and leave you once you do not have any more. There is a saying I heard once that still stands true- People come into your life for two reasons, to give or to take. You must prepare yourself for how you will deal with these people when they come because you need both to function and survive. So your first goal needs to be to work on you and finding out what makes you happy.

Secondly, you need to reexamine the criteria you use to determine the type of man you want. Stop looking for men to be with and work on what you desire and want from a ideally realistic man for you. Ideally being the image that you have of the perfect man and realistic meaning excluding the factors that make the ideal man unattainable. Stop sharing yourself (having sex) with everyone that appears to be a good choice or you may never get to or experience the right one when he comes along.

You may not consider yourself promiscuous but if you continue to engage in the act of those that do then how would anyone tell the difference.

We all have a personal responsibility to ourselves to carry ourselves in the way that honors our Significant other even before they come along. Yes, we screw it up from time to time on those we think are worth it only to find out later they aren't, but that does not give us a permission slip to throw all sense of responsibility out the window. You have to think highly of yourself and carry yourself the way you want others to treat you. If you do these things then you will not be concerned with whether you are the only one between the "two walls" of your home because it would be by choice if you are not… by default.

Dear Ask the Man,

My name is nothing but a fool,

Hello Ask the man. I can't believe I'm writing you as I have fallen on pure desperation. I once was in a painful and abusive relationship with a man who was twelve years younger than me. I don't know what the hell I was ever thinking when getting involved. My only initial thought was to have one sexual encounter with him then move on, but of course, he had an alternative motive. I don't know how or when, but this guy winded up being one of my dependents. I gave him everything as far as financial and emotional support. I know I should have known better, right? He told me he loved me and wanted to marry me. What a fool I was to ever think he would ever want me as an older wife. After his physical and verbal abuse, I decided to end the relationship. Well, it's been almost a year and I have moved on and I'm in a better relationship with a guy who's just the opposite of this joker. However, when I see him or hear things about him, it makes me literally sick. Ask the man, I want to be free from these painful memories that subject me to being a bitter woman. I'm certain he hasn't lost any sleep over this. I have prayed on it but maybe I haven't prayed hard enough. Ask the man; please tell me what I should do at this point.

Dear Reader,

Thank you for writing in. The purpose of "Ask the Man" is to enlighten, educate, and empower. With that being said, please allow me to start off by saying you are not a fool. We all have made some unwise decisions that upon looking back were not our greatest moments but the mere fact that you wrote to ask for enlightenment on your situation separates you from those considered to be foolish. Foolishness is recognizing that you need help but refusing to ask for it.

Secondly, although we don't choose who we fall in love with, we can position ourselves in a way to better project possible positive results. In other words, not set ourselves up for failure. When you met the younger man, you were so infatuated with someone his age and stature showing interest in you that you ignored the normal process of rationalization. It is because of this you failed to notice that you were unequally yoked. Sexual relations simply helped cloud things further. Once this occurred, the physical and verbal abuse began. You did forget one. He also mentally abused you.

When most relationships end, the physical and verbal abuse stops but the mental abuse or anger continues. The reason you, like so many others, cannot be happy with someone else, even though you claim you are no longer in love with the person that did you so wrong and despite you having moved on to other relationships with other people is because a chapter in your book of life was not closed properly. You must address the root of your problem. Although you have separated yourself physically from him, you are still allowing him to influence your thought process. Every time you are about to make a decision you pause and think on what he would say or think. This is because you have not forgiven him. Forgiveness is for you not anyone else. Tyler Perry explained this in one of the best ways I have heard it put lately. When you fail to forgive someone, you give them power over you. The way you determine if you fall in this category is to ask yourself, does the very mention of his name change your mood? Does your skin quiver when they come around? Do you constantly compare anyone you deal with to them? If you answered yes to any or all of these questions, they have a power over you. The only way to relinquish this power is to forgive them. Let the things that they did to you go. Not only him, but also forgive yourself. Many times we forgive others but don't forgive ourselves. We walk around with pain and resentment all built up inside. You must let it go and move on with your life. This is a process and it does not mean you will never think of them or wish things had turned out differently but that chapter and season in your life is over and you must move on. When you pray, ask for forgiveness for both yourself and him. Then ask to cast your memories into the sea of forgetfulness. We often say we can forgive but can't forget. This is because our responsibility is only to forgive and allow the creator to handle the forgetfulness part. Life is about experiences, learn from them and use them to better your future decisions. Good luck!

Chapter 5

Communication is the Key

In our previous chapters we discussed the importance of learning yourself before attempting to tackle the challenge of learning someone else and exploring the complexity of your mind and life. Many people have asked me what they should do if they are involved with someone and how do they know if they should quit and search for something else. If this is you then this moment is for you. If you are in a situation where you have been questioning if your significant other or the special someone you are "eyeing" will ever come around, then you have come to the right corner and this "stitch" is for you.

Have you ever seen someone you were interested in and the first thing that crossed your mind was who you were going to cheat on them with or if there was anybody better that was waiting around the corner? I am pretty sure you looked at the previous sentence sideways because it appears to not be the normal way of thinking. When you first come across someone you believe will interest you, your thought process is to explore the opportunity, not look around for other options that may come. Unfortunately many times this is what we find ourselves doing. We see opportunities as work. We don't want to put forth the effort or go through the process in order to reap the rewards of that opportunity. We have become a microwave society. We want everything yesterday and look to gain the greatest rewards for the least amount of investment. This is the core reason as to why we cannot seem to find happiness and we jump from one false anomaly to the next.

Many times, we set ourselves up for failure from the beginning. Although the sentence that began the previous paragraph seemed absurd, many people do it every day. Let us take a guy named Paul for example. He saw this bright, very attractive, entry level executive who seemed to have a lot going for herself. After asking around, he found out she was not seeing anyone but was somewhat old fashion. She had morals and strong beliefs, yet Paul felt she was the one for him. After meeting and going out for several months, the reality of her being the "one you take home to meet momma" set in but Paul began watching and listening to others and started believing he was not ready to settle down. While she, on the other hand, began talking about where they would live, how many kids they may have, he started daydreaming and mind-wondering. Instead of communicating this to her, he began to string her along, not calling and being less and less available; eventually beginning to look around for other opportunities, I mean women. (Small joke). Does this sound normal?

The problem with most people is not that they cannot find someone to be with but rather they do not know what to do when they do have someone in their life. It's easy to say all things we would do if we were in a relationship when we are single but then when we are with someone most of us find fifty million excuses as to why we do not do hardly any of the things we said we would do. The problem starts with communication. Neither partner is willing to do everything that is necessary to fix the issue. Most people mean well and if you ask them, are willing to do some things when given the chance to get to the bottom of their issues. But actually solving their problems have to do with them exploring every possibility. This, they are not really too excited about. This part of the process cannot be completed without communication. We have a tendency to only tell others what we want them to know or what is convenient for us. Three things must be done in order to establish, maintain, and continue a successful relationship with someone regarding communication.

The first is full disclosure. Ok, so I know many of you are shaking your head right now and saying you cannot disclose everything about yourself because your partner might not choose to be with you anymore. Most people think of full disclosure as unto a dump truck pulling up and unloading all of its garbage at one time. This is not what I am saying. No one is prepared for this. Rather I am suggesting that you be like a concrete truck. When a concrete truck comes to unload its cement, it is constantly turning just as we should constantly be evolving. Before the concrete can be dumped, the driver takes the time to meet with the cement mason or cement finisher; they are the one who receives the concrete off the truck and spreads it out evenly. When a concrete truck goes to dump, it does so a little at a time, dispensing only what the cement finishers can handle. This is just how open we should be in relationships. We need to express to our partners that there are things that we will tell them up front that we feel they need to be aware of. Some we may forget and others will just come to the surface later. This is because you had a life before them and it is going to take time to reveal everything about yourself to them. We need to prepare them and ask them to be open as these things come out. It is also important to express that in exchange you will be open to things revealed about them over time as well. The key to this is understanding that just as we all have a past before we get with someone, we are also constantly evolving into who we are to become and this should be viewed as the spice that keeps each partner interested not the strains that tear you apart.

The second communication factor is what I call an "exchangeable understanding". Many times our partner does what we view as incomprehensible and we refuse to move past it. The truth is we have all or will eventually find ourselves in a position where we risk the trust of our partner. We have to be willing to view circumstances as if you switched places with them. How would you want your partner to act? Give you another chance or release you from your commitments to move on with your life? Yes, I did just suggest possible break up. Unfortunately people make the mistake of staying with someone when they have decided in their heart they were done way back in the relationship. Don't waste each other's time. *STITCHES # 118 - If you are going to give it a shot, have an exchangeable heart and try to understand what is needed to move past the moment.* Notice I said to understand what is needed to move on and not to necessarily understand why what happened occurred. Many make this mistake. We get so caught up on the why it happened, we cannot see past it and just like a wound not tended to but rather picked at, it becomes infected and worse. Everyone knows an infected wound that is not tended to properly can result in a total loss. One must stay focused and see past the moment, whether that is together or apart. This has to be communicated as soon as you come to a conclusion. Both partners deserve to not spend unnecessary time putting work into something when the other is over and done. Let's be honest, we all know when we are done or when we are just trying to make a stink to get our point across.

Lastly, is a willingness to learn as you move forward. Communication is a two way door and each partner holds their own master key. Your master key only works for your side. When you use it in an attempt to gain access to someone else, you must understand that your door jamb must be removed in order to get full use of your access. A door jamb is what you find in most doors that keep it from swinging both ways. In communication, we often like to access other people but do not want them having full access to us. This is not how it works. Communication is essential for any relationship to flourish. It is the number one reason why marriages and relationships fail. Before cheating and financial woos, communication is the beginning of it all. Not just by the lack of communication but not handling situations correctly after the information is brought to the forefront. A person must be willing to be open, call things as they are, and be willing to work through their moments no matter what they are. Resolutions will be achieved, the question is just at what cost.

Generate a Personal Desire to Experience Success

The age old saying that you can take a horse to the water but you cannot make him drink still applies today. You can teach a person what it takes to be successful, give them the tools, and even help them get started but the decision is ultimately on them as to whether they use the tools and if they desire to experience success. Many people claim to want it, swear they will do whatever it takes to get it but then instantaneously switch to whatever excuse is available to explain why they do not have success and are not continually working toward it. I heard a story once of a young man who said he wanted to be a success. He sought out a teacher/mentor who agreed to share his knowledge with him. The teacher asked the student if he really wanted to be a success and just how far he was willing to go to obtain it. The boy smeared and said he would do whatever. The teacher told him to meet him on the beach the next morning. The young man shrugged not understanding completely but agreed to meet him. The next morning shortly before day break the young man arrived to the beach wearing his best suit as he believed dressing for success was the answer. When he arrived he found the teacher/mentor in a small boat. As soon as the young man reached the edge of the water, without saying any words but motioning with his hands for him to stay there, the teacher pushes off from the shore. Once about thirty feet from the shore, the teacher calls out to the young man saying, "How bad do you want to be successful?" The young man yells back, "That's why I'm here". The teacher/mentor replied with "Come On" and motioned for the student to come in his direction with his hands. The young man looked around for another boat but did not see one. He humped his shoulders and looks at the older man who was still beckoning for him to come. The young man was still in deep thought processes when the man in the boat interrupted his dialogue with himself with an outburst, "Get in the water". The student looked confused but began to walk. The water began to rise; first to his ankles and then to his knees and hips. The young man soon realized that as he was getting closer, the teacher was gradually drifting away from him. The student turned to go back but the teacher yelled out again, "How bad do you want it?". The young man continued and eventually the water was to the young man's neck and he was treading water. When he got to the boat he reached out for the teacher to give him a hand into the boat but instead the teacher pushed his head down under the water. Grasping for breath, the teacher release his head to allow the young man to catch his breath but the young man just came up hollering, "What is wrong with you man? Are you trying to kill me?". The teacher pushed his head back under the water. This continued two or three more times until the young man stopped yelling and just started catching his breath as the teacher allowed him to come up for air. Each time the teacher kept saying, "How bad do you want?" The young man finally answered, "I want it so bad I cannot breathe you silly old man." With that the teacher/mentor pulled the young man into the boat. He said now you are ready to learn. The essential lessons everyone must know about success is that it may not come the way you expect it, it may come by way of uncharted waters, you cannot allow the idea of being overwhelmed to overtake you, and you have to want success as vitally as you want to breath. It all starts with you and your thought process.

Chapter 6

It Starts with Self

Have you ever felt your love life was like a roller coaster? Has it often left you with a sense of nausea that makes you never want to visit another theme park, let alone chance any more rides. Well, if this sounds like you and you need change then you have reached the right corner. In the Stitches' Corner, we will discuss how you can best prepare yourself for success before, during, and between relationships. Just like roller coasters are meant to have its ups and downs, jerks and turns, so are relationships. The dreams of living in a big house with a white picket fence and no issues are far from reality. That is just a dream. Reality has twist and turns. There are two major issues that many face when it comes to relationships as they relate to a roller coaster - 1) recognizing what you are supposed to take away from the ride and 2) realizing when it is time to get off and move on. The key is not to turn down the side effects of the ride, but rather to learn from every episode so that your next ride will be more productive; therefore, eventually getting to the place where the ride is actually something you look forward to. When you take a roller coaster ride, your heart is pumping and your adrenaline is racing. The ride has left you with lasting effects and memories. At this point is where riders begin to differ. Some go right back and stand in lines, for hours even, just for another three minute thrill, while others are off to the next ride, we will discuss them in a minute. Learning from a situation is not just limited to when you are moving from one person to another but also when dealing with the same person. The first part of this process is learning to address inflictions or wounds. These may be present tense or past. Just like physically, from time to time, having wounds that are so deep simply putting a band-aid on it will not do very much. This is where doctors will often use stitches. Their purpose is to hold the wound together long enough for the nature healing process to occur. This same rule applies to relationships and is where the concept of "stitches" derived. Relationships often need the same level of care and attention. The roller coaster that seems to have either drained us or left us with untold scares and wounds are what I like to called the "love experience". Unfortunately, no one ever told you this ride has several side effects including but not limited to total disgust and exhaustion. Not so long ago I was talking with someone who could not understand why they were experiencing the problems they were encountering in their present relationship. As I listen to their story, I began to hear how she had just gone from one relationship experience to next, repeating many of the same experiences. I recalled my mom telling me when I first separated from my ex-wife that I needed to take time for me to get my ex "out of my system". Like most children, I heard my mother but did not listen. I started dating someone and it turned into a disaster pretty quickly. I had so many pinned up emotions from my marriage that, looking back, I can remember the girl I was seeing at the time saying, "I can't seem to do nothing right and I don't know how to please you". The worst part was I saw her trying and quite frankly, at the time, I heard myself say, "I don't care and I'm not asking you to stick around". This might sound familiar. Too many of us take baggage from previous rides or encounters with us to the next, thinking that if we just satisfy the emotional or physical element, then everything would be just fine. Unfortunately, it does not work that way. There has to be a time of reflection and preparation. Here we will teach you how to create a better you, thus changing the dynamics of how you interact with others.

This leads us to the other type of thrill seekers that are so infatuated with a three minute ride that they will repeat it over and over, even after the original thrill is gone. I knew a couple once that asked my opinion on whether or not they should continue to pursue their relationship. After hearing their story, meeting with them several times, and watching how they interacted with each other, my personal opinion was drastically different from my professional one. They had all the clear signs that the relationship was over and they were just putting up with each other because of kids and convenience. I always tell people that my job is not to tell you what to do or make decisions for your relationship. I'm here to help if you see what you may not have seen previously and face decisions you need to address but have been unwilling to do alone. The real truth about people, like this couple, is they only put up a smoke screen about wanting to make their relationship work. They are a ticking time bomb that will eventually explode into what will leave their lives distorted and in too many unrecoverable pieces. I chose to stop advising the couple because they really did not want help. They only wanted someone outside of each other to hear their arguments. They had spent so much time talking to what became deaf ears when they went to each other that it was no longer worth it anymore. This happens all too often and is one of the reasons partners resort to seeking gratification from an outside party. I tried repeatedly to help the couple understand the importance of starting with themselves. Looking for a partner to make you whole is the wrong answer. It does not work. Plus, you will not find anyone who does have everything. No matter how many times I stressed it, I could not get the couple to get this major concept: The key to finding true happiness with someone is looking inside yourself as opposed to and before looking inside others.

STITCHES #5- It starts with Self - Learn to Love You. We live in a day and age where everything is about the gratification of others and what they think. What will my friends think if I break up with what they see as this great guy? Should I stick it out? He says if I really love him, I would do this or do that with and for him. The list of scenarios could go on for days. The point is that in many cases we let our world revolve around other people's ideologies. In a sense, we begin to mimic what we want people to see and think so much, people get our representative instead of our true self. To change this, we must start learning to love ourselves. To do this, we must begin by getting to know ourselves. It might seem strange but get in front of a mirror, look at your reflection eye to eye and introduce yourself. From there, ask yourself questions about what makes you who you are. Give yourself some time alone and fall in love with that person. Then, when you introduce anyone else to that person, you will be less likely to compromise the love you already have for yourself with a blind love that does not know what it truly wants or where it is going.

Sometimes it may feel like you are running down a dark lonely road filled with fogginess and midst. Many cars are passing but no one is stopping for you. The more you cry and seem to plead for help, the faster they seem to speed by. A couple of times you've even thought to throw yourself in the way of a few of those who pass by but cannot seem to pull yourself to suicide just yet. The road that you are on is filled with buildings with lights on but it just does not seem that any will answer you. You know that there are people inside because you can hear them but it is as though they cannot hear you. Although this scenario is fictitious, the feelings are real. The answers that you seek are not any place you look nor can they be found by others who pass you as they are headed to their destination. The answers are within. Before you can truly be loved or love someone else, you have to love yourself. You have to be able to look in the mirror and say "Self, I love me some you".

I know this may not seem like anything new and it is not meant to be. The problem we have is not that we do not know the answers that we seek all the time but rather we lack the extra necessary to make them a reality for us. We watch people all the time who are happy and then others who appear to be and sometimes neither seem very different to us. We in turn try to mimic what they appear to have but it does not work out for us. The answers are within us. Learn who you are, learn what you want, generate a personal desire to experience it, and place yourself in the way of success.

Chapter 7

Learn Who You Are

What do you see when you look in the mirror? Do you recognize the figure staring back at you? If you really look closely, is it who you really are? Is the outside reflective of the inside?

Learning who you are is vital to learning what you should be looking for and understanding what you end up with purposely or unintentionally. Let us begin with unintentionally. Most people end up with someone unintentionally when they were really out to get something specifically. When I asked a group of people in a survey I did to tell me the characteristics they look for in a partner, the answers were repetitive. They all listed things like someone who is nice, hard-working, trustworthy, dependable, etc. These are all wonderful traits but when I asked a smaller group to list the attributes they bring to the table, their list was significantly smaller then what many of them had just listed as things they look for. My point behind this is that we look for traits that we ourselves have not developed and then we wonder why we cannot pick a partner who can get it right. I often tell people that if you are not prepared to offer more than you expect to receive, then you need to continue working on you for a while longer before adding someone else to your gumbo.

So, how do you learn yourself? I was talking to a friend recently and we were talking about relationships and how she had grand plans to find the perfect person. But when I asked her how she prepared for meeting them and where she planned to find this person, she was clueless. When I offered the suggestion of starting by learning herself, she got silent. I took her silence as a sign of not understanding what I was referring to so I continued on to explain. I asked her to tell me about herself as if I was a new person that she had not known. I ask her what she would be comfortable sharing upfront to a stranger. She told me all the basic information; her age, family importance, some minor interest, and what she looks for in a man. I then asked how much she knew about herself. She paused and looked at me kind of funny like before finally asking me what I meant. We spend countless hours telling others what we think they want to hear or what we deem important that they need to hear up front but if both partners are doing this, then there is a whole lot that is simply not shared which most people will agree become vital information that we all wish we would have known earlier later down the line.

Learning yourself is about breaking this process down to its lowest common factors. Below are what I believe are the top 101 character traits we all need to know about ourselves. They are broken down into sections. As you go through the questions, you should write them down.

STITCHES: The Foundation

1) What is your full name? Do you have a middle name?
2) Where and when were you born?
3) Who are/were your parents? (Know their names, occupations, personalities, etc.)
4) Do you have any siblings? What are/were they like? (Know their names, occupations, personalities, etc.)
5) Do you own or rent? Where do you live now and with whom? Describe the place and the person/people.
6) What is your occupation? Is it what you planned to be?
7) Write a full physical description of yourself. You might want to consider factors such as: height, weight, race, hair and eye color, style of dress, and any tattoos, scars, or distinguishing marks.
8) To which social class do you belong?

9) Do you have any allergies, diseases, or other physical weaknesses?

10) Are you right- or left-handed?

11) What words and/or phrases do you use very frequently?

12) Do you have any quirks, strange mannerisms, annoying habits, or other defining characteristics?

STITCHES: Growing Up

13) How would you describe your childhood in general?

14) What is your earliest memory?

15) How much schooling have you had?

16) Did you enjoy school?

17) Where did you learn most of your skills and other abilities?

18) While growing up, did you have any role models? If so, describe them.

19) While growing up, how did you get along with the other members of your family?

20) As a child, what did you want to be when you grew up?

21) As a child, what were your favorite activities?

22) As a child, what kinds of personality traits did you display?

23) As a child, were you popular? Who were your friends, and what were they like?

24) When and with whom was your first kiss?

25) Are you a virgin? If not, when and with whom did you lose your virginity?

26) Describe any influences in your past that led you to do the things you do today.

STITCHES: Past Influences

27) What do you consider the most important event of your life so far?

28) Who has had the most influence on you?

29) What do you consider your greatest achievement?

30) What is your greatest regret?

31) What is the most evil thing you have ever done?

32) Do you have a criminal record of any kind?

33) When was the time you were the most frightened?

34) What is the most embarrassing thing that ever happened to you?

35) If you could change one thing from your past, what would it be, and why?

36) What is your best memory?

37) What is your worst memory?

STITCHES: Beliefs and Opinions

38) Are you basically optimistic or pessimistic?

39) What is your greatest fear?

40) What are your religious views?

41) What are your political views?

42) What are your views on sex?

43) Are you able to kill? Under what circumstances do you find killing to be acceptable or unacceptable?

44) In your opinion, what is the most evil thing any human being could do?

45) Do you believe in the existence of soul mates and/or true love?

46) What do you believe makes a successful life?

47) How honest are you about your thoughts and feelings (i.e. do you hide your true self from others, and in what way)?

48) Do you have any biases or prejudices?

49) Is there anything you absolutely refuse to do under any circumstances? Why do you refuse to do it?

50) Who or what, if anything, would you die for (or otherwise go to extremes for)?

STITCHES: Relationships with Others

51) In general, how do you treat others (politely, rudely, by keeping them at a distance, etc.)? Does your treatment of them change depending on how well you know them, and if so, how?

52) Who is the most important person in your life, and why?

53) Who is the person you respect the most, and why?

54) Who are your friends? Do you have a best friend? Describe these people.

55) Do you have a spouse or significant other? If so, describe this person.

56) Have you ever been in love? If so, describe what happened.

57) What do you look for in a potential lover?

58) How close are you to your family?

59) Have you started your own family? If so, describe them. If not, do you want to? Why or why not?

60) Who would you turn to if you were in desperate need of help?

61) Do you trust anyone to protect you? Who, and why?

62) If you died or went missing, who would miss you?

63) Who is the person you despise the most, and why?

64) Do you tend to argue with people, or avoid conflict?

65) Do you tend to take on leadership roles in social situations?

66) Do you like interacting with large groups of people? Why or why not?

67) Do you care what others think of you?

STITCHES: Favorites

68) What is/are your favorite hobbies and pastimes?

69) What is your most treasured possession?

70) What is your favorite color?

71) What is your favorite food?

72) What, if anything, do you like to read?

73) What is your idea of good entertainment (consider music, movies, art, etc.)?

74) Do you smoke, drink, or use drugs? If so, why? Do you want to quit?

75) How do you spend a typical Saturday night?

76) What makes you laugh?

77) What, if anything, shocks or offends you?

78) What would you do if you had insomnia and had to find something to do to amuse yourself?

79) How do you deal with stress?

80) Are you spontaneous or do you always need to have a plan?

81) What are your pet peeves?

82) Which type of vacation do you prefer?

    a. Sun, fun, and relax

    b. Sightseeing

    c. Outdoor adventure

83) The best type of gift for me is something:

    a. Practical

    b. Sentimental

    c. Just what they asked for

    d. A surprise

STITCHES: Selfie

84) Describe the routine of a normal day for you. How do you feel when this routine is disrupted?

85) What is your greatest strength as a person?

86) What is your greatest weakness?

87) If you could change one thing about yourself, what would it be?

88) Are you generally introverted or extroverted?

89) Are you generally organized or messy?

90) Name three things you consider yourself to be very good at, and three things you consider yourself to be very bad at.

91) Do you like yourself?

92) What are your reasons for being an adventurer (or doing the strange and heroic things that characters do)? Are your real reasons for doing this different than the ones you tell people in public? (If so, detail both sets of reasons...)

93) What goal do you most want to accomplish in your lifetime?

94) Where do you see yourself in 5 years?

95) If you could choose, how would you want to die?

96) If you knew you were going to die in 24 hours, name three things you would do in the time you had left.

97) What is the one thing for which you would most like to be remembered after your death?

98) What three words best describe your personality?

99) What three words would others probably use to describe you?
100) If you could offer yourself advice on your life up unto this point, what would that advice be?
101) What advice would you offer someone else?

Chapter 8

Is Love Alone Enough?

Tina Turner sang a song that has made people wonder the full gravity of its meaning for years. The song's title "What's Love Got to Do with It", makes you ask if love is but a second hand emotion. This means that there are factors at work which are of much deeper concern and meaning then the simple idea of love. Too many times people get caught up in the glamour and prestige of being in "love". If you ask them they will say and even put on such a front that others would not know any different. All the while, they are miserable and with feelings of regret. The answer to this riddle, if I might call it, is to simply know your happiness level. Most people only concern themselves with the sacrificial necessities of life. They want to feel love but do not know what it means to really be happy and in love. They go hand in hand. You cannot have love without happiness. Happiness is a personal. You must achieve inner happiness before being able to share or provide the experience with anyone else. You cannot fake this. When you go by someone else's version of happiness it causes you to act outside of yourself and thus causing you and others around you to be affected negativity. The way it affects you is not necessarily the way you expect it to. For instance, when you find yourself having dated several people who on the surface appear ideal but either you fail to fulfill them or you feel like there should be more. So the cycle continues and you move on to the next person. Eventually you figure you are doomed and the perfect fit for you simply does not exist and you settle for someone less then you deserve, equaling your misery or you decide to stop even trying. This is all because you defined your happiness and your view of love through the scopes of those around you.

A dear friend helped me to understand this concept fully and I'm going to use it to help you understand risk. It comes down to cost and depreciation value. My friend asked parenthetically, to herself, just out loud (like so many of us do), why do people buy a vehicle and then turn around and trade it in a short time later and expect to get what they put into the car back. What many people fail to understand is the depreciation process. When a vehicle is purchased, it loses its value the second it is driven off the lot. Regardless of whether it was driven up to a hundred miles or a hundred thousand, the value of the vehicle still goes down.

Just like with a car, there is a risk involved in just about every action and every decision. We all take risks every day. We take risks on others and others take risks on us. We risk things every time we get into a car, stop at stop signs, red lights, or simply by riding down the road. The risk is not only what we do but what other people do as well. Then, of course, there are the other factors that we have very little to no control over that weigh in heavily on the value or outcome of things as well. Nevertheless, to take a risk, one must have faith. Risks can be viewed as an opportunity. An opportunity is nothing more than a chance. People take and use these things every day. The moment we are born we began to depreciate in value. Whether it is the countless partners we have allowed to share our body pleasures or the abuse and torture from experiencing day to day struggles and trials. Some of them are greater than others but nevertheless, risky. Risky because the short or long term effects cannot be managed or accurately predicted. Whether it is the woman who is happily married with kids but cannot seem to keep her legs closed from every man that looks or makes her feel special or the man who sleeps around because he cannot commit.

On the flip side of that, we are all risks. Someone took a chance on us. Some risks work out well and the worth is greater thereafter; others, not so much. Some of us would now just consider ourselves damaged goods. When you meet someone and consider spending "quality" time with them in an effort to grow closer to each other, they are taking a risk. It is a risk because it requires time and regardless of whether you agree or not, time is your most valuable asset. It is intangible and irreplaceable. No one wants to waste their time but yet many of us do it willingly every day. Say for instance, Sam has met Sue and although initially Sue appears to be more hesitant than Sam, they both recognize that there are risks at stake. For Sam, he risks his manhood, time, and esteem. For Sam, his manhood is viewed as his pride in being a provider and leader in the relationship. For Sue, she is risking her livelihood, time, and esteem. With regards to her livelihood, Sue understands that her main goal is to look for a way to provide long term for herself and a possible future family. If you notice, they both are risking similar things otherwise but one is more concerned about self-image than the other. Now do not get me wrong, I am not man bashing, you have to understand that being a provider is a learned behavior. The natural side of a man desires to jump off a cliff and do other dare devilish stunts. They are but smoke and mirrors to pride and self-preservation.

Being a man who takes care of someone else is a behavior picked up and conditioned with life experiences. The problem with so many men is that they learned from someone just imitating the act of being a man. Every species learns to be who it is by following in the footsteps of an older like model. Well, what happens when there fails to be a sufficient model to follow behind? We end up in a society much like what we have today. Babies have kids and folks are reluctant to take any responsibilities while they point the figures at other people and blame them for their shortcomings.

The next concept relative to a vehicle again is insurance. Some people drive their entire lives and never get into so much as a fender bender but yet they pay thousands of dollars a year for "just in case assurance". That is what I call assurance, just in case something happens insurance. I heard a comedian say it once, if the purpose of insurance is so that just in case something happens, what if nothing happens? Shouldn't you get something back? These are legitimate questions. But what the comedian did not know was that shareholders in the company do receive revenue when accidents are down and in turn do receive money back. Well yes, you were just thinking it, how we relate to ourselves and others can be viewed as insurance to Hope....it's a word that we all share but it does not belong to any of us.....or does it? The reasons I ask this question is because how many times do you find yourself hopeless because someone else has dropped the ball? Or even worse, you have. If hope is not dependent upon someone else, then why are we so quick to say it is gone and we are hopeless? Take for instance, a friend or even worse, a potential mate is supposed to meet you at a restaurant. You take them at their word and have made all arrangements to be there and on time. Due to traffic, you call or text to let them know you will be running late and at first there is no response. Then, somewhere around ten minutes before your scheduled appointment, they text and say they will not be able to make it and can you reschedule. Now allow me to be boisterous for a moment on behalf of any and everybody that has ever experienced this rude and inconsiderate act. Unplanned events and emergencies happen in our lives every day but although emergencies, naturally are unplanned, are excusable from missing engagements, being late, or not contacting the person or persons previously scheduled appointments are with; simple unplanned events are a totally separate issue entirely. There is no excuse. This is the twenty first century and with as much technology as we have today, to not notify people when you have an unplanned event to happen is inconsiderate. These are the types of things that cause people to lose hope in others. I mean faith or trust. They all go hand and hand. When you tell someone you are going to do something or be somewhere, you do it. You never know what is at stake. Someone is counting on you to be the person they can count on. It goes back to the age old saying that we are to treat people as you would want to be treated. How did you feel the last time someone dropped the ball on you. Those same sentiments are what you should think about when dealing with others. It is never funny when the shoe is on your foot. What may appear amusing or no big deal on your end may be a life changer for someone else. It only takes one wrong move. If you do not think it is as serious as I appear to be making it. Then ask yourself, how many people that co-worker who committed suicide last year or that pre-teen who exploded at school not long ago tried to reach out to but everybody was so caught up in their own agenda that they did not notice their light dwindling. Hope is much like faith; we are all born with at least a little bit. You can view it just as you would a candle. When you are born the candle is lit. Certain things in your life can help strengthen your fire. On the contrary, as we experience some people and things our hope has a tendency to be sabotaged by them. Sometimes they know it and do not care enough to stop and other times they seem to suck the air out of us and cause our light to go dim. The major problem with not prioritizing the people we encounter is that you never know just how close they are to the edge. The solution is to treat everyone as if they are close to the edge. When you see that student who seems to not have a friend in the world and all of sudden they start dressing different and doing out of the ordinary stuff which others find comical, take some time and show them some attention. When you see that coworker who is witnessing their whole world come down on them and it does not seem to be anything they can do, offer to help. It just may change their world. We all have to take turns experiencing trials and strife. As I often hear Ministers say, although it is there day today, it could be yours tomorrow.

Then there is the other side. What do you do if it is your hope which is lost? How do you get it back? You have the power to control your destiny. Many times our failure comes when we give too much power to others. Folks and things can only leave you hopeless if you give them all your hope. Now do not misunderstand me. I am not saying to never trust anyone and to walk around being all about you. You have to understand that people only in your life for a season and a reason. There are no time limits or expirations to the seasons so do not get hung up on the time segments. Focus on the reasons. I once knew someone that I saw so much in. I wanted to be around them twenty- four seven, three sixty five. I was not sure why I wanted to be around them so much but I did. We all know people like this. I was asked by several people why I hung out with them but I could not answer for myself. It was not until the nature of our relationship changed that I saw what made me desire to hang out with them so much. There are some people that you will meet which have the ability to make you feel like you are on top of the world and that you can achieve whatever you aspire to. Unfortunately sometimes we misunderstand and do not understand the reason until the season is over. That person was placed in my life to give me the drive to dream. I will forever be in the debt of them for giving me that. That was only part of the tools I needed to get where I am now, however. Before the season was over, I began to try and carry the season into my next and it in turned could have caused major implications. I saw potential in them but it was really a reflection of the potential in me. There are some people you will meet who are intended to just be cheerleaders in your life as you move toward your destiny. You must be careful not to think they are players because although they are gifted, it is for their sport and placing them in your arena can only disrupt progress and distract you from your goals. I spent so much time focusing on what I thought was their potential and not working on mine that I actually sidelined mine and my game stopped altogether. For years I blamed it on them and stood stagnant but the truth is that I caused my own shortfalls. They were cheering me on and I kept trying to get them to come play the game, my game. It is like a quarterback in football going to the sideline and urging a cheerleader to stop cheering and come get in the game. All the while, the cheerleader was fulfilling her purpose.

Most people look at their failure in relationships as a sign that they do not know what they are doing and that the outcome is due to some fatal mistake they have made. In actuality, the relationship many times over was doomed way before it even began. The same way you should not expect to go into a room blind and not to run into a wall or two, you cannot take the attitude of however the chips fall is the way you will handle it when it comes to relationships.

One of America's favorite pastimes is watching professional sports. We do not watch it for the mistakes or because we do not have anything else to do, we watch it to see who is going to make the least amount of mistakes. Who is going to go into it with the best game plan? Who's going to execute their game plan with the least amount of errors? The truth of the matter is most of the time we select our favorite team on this same thesis; hence the reason why it does not matter to some if their favorite team is not the home town or state team. I can remember listening to several of my friends post on their media statuses how disgusted they were at how their team was performing in a "must" win. They were so disturbed that they were scouring the channels in search of something if not anything more interesting to entertain them and take their minds off that they were made to witness.

Unfortunately we treat our relationships with this same degree of misfortune. When I asked a group of random people when did they determine the characteristics of the person they we looking to be with, more times over I got the response of after they meet someone and had started dating them. In writing this book I want to make two things clear. I believe that people are put in our lives for a reason and there is no such thing as failure unless you ignore the lesson or lessons that should have come from them. There are things we can do to better prepare us for that which will inevitably come.

Chapter 9

Learn What You Want: Creating an Executable Plan

Have you ever taken yourself to the movies? What about to a restaurant or your favorite show? If you have never done these things or stuff like it then how do you know what to tell someone who is trying to court or date you? You must know what you want if you ever expect someone else to learn what those things are and do them for and to you. Let me say it this way *STITCHES # 2 - I have to know what makes me tick before I can teach anyone else how I tick or keep them from ticking me off.* The only way to successfully do this is by taking the time before you introduce someone into the equation and simply learn your thought process and desires. *STITCHES #81 - You must know what an image looks like in order to identify its reflection.*

Some time ago I was asked to speak to a group of young people concerning what they should be looking for in a mate. I have to be honest and say it kind of caught me off guard because I thought up until five minutes before speaking to them that I was addressing a totally separate issue altogether. When I was told the topic, I gasped to myself and when they asked if it was going to be a problem I nonchalantly said no and I would come up with something. I will honestly say I was at a lost. My mind was blank and I was racking it to figure out what to say and where to start. Once I got in front of everyone I started by asking what they were looking for. The answers varied but were nothing out of the norm. Someone physically attractive, intelligent, trustworthy, understanding, and the list went on and on. In a way they were repeating themselves but just using different words. I then asked what they brought to the table. Of course, they listed some things but not as extensive as the list of qualities they are looking for their mate to have. Here is where I found one of the first problems we have when we look for a companion, we look for them to be developed with all these features and characteristics, in a way a resume with plenty of experience but when asked by the interviewed what we offer, the interviewer, have but a couple of attributes to offer.

I instructed the group to do something I feel anyone looking to find a mate needs to do: Create a "Living Relationship Forecaster". A Living Relationship Forecaster (LRF) is a tool used to determine what a person looks for in a relationship; what they bring to the table and what they are and are not comfortable with when it comes to a partner and their actions. This LRF is but a guide. Every person is different and thus what we look for will vary as well. The LRF is composed of two parts. Completing it before you ever begin dating anyone is most useful but it can be beneficial in any stage of the relationship. There are two parts. Part one describes the type of person you are and part two describes the progression of the relationship. I cannot reiterate how important it is that these exercises be done before someone is brought into the mix. If you are already involved with someone, do not fret, this only means you need to be more careful with your decisions at this point.

Part one of the LRF is the relationship plan. Take a sheet of paper, doesn't matter the size, as long as you can fold it into four parts. On the first side label one section "Qualities Desired". In this section list all of the features and characteristics that you are looking for. This paper is for your eyes only so there should not be any issues with honesty. List all of the characteristics you are looking for, whether physically, emotionally, spiritually, financially, intellectually, or whatever. Examples are God fearing, at least 5'10 but no taller than 6'1, athletic build, loves to workout but is not obsessed, financially independent, has a legal job with health insurance and benefits, loves children, is close to his family but not too close, and has their own place to live, etc. I believe you get the idea. Take your time, there is no rush or limit. If you run out of space, just get another sheet of paper.

The next section should be labeled "Self Attributes". These are the qualities or characteristics in which you believe you bring to the relationship. Don't sell yourself short in this section because doing so will only limit you giving yourself worthwhile credit later. These are not just characteristics that you know of but those others suggest about you as well. Examples of this will vary depending on what you feel you bring to the table. Think this part through very carefully as it may very well be the most important part. Ask yourself things like are you an understanding person and what makes people want to be around you. If you do not have anything for this, then you need to start working on it.

On the back side of your paper are two other sections. Label one of them "Deal With". Here is where you list all of the things you can see yourself dealing with that a partner could come to the relationship with. Again, this is going to vary from person to person because what one person is willing to deal with, another may not see as a problem at all or may be unwilling to deal with all together. This leads me to the last section. It is called "Roll Out". After reading the other sections, this part is pretty self-explanatory. This is where you list all of the characteristics which would bring an immediate or abrupt end to a relationship. I cannot give examples for this section because they do vary from person to person and the whole idea of this is to help you understand yourself.

Chapter 10

A Realistic Vantage Point

When it comes to finding an ideal match for our lives, we should not do a piss poor job at the thought, planning and attention we give to it. There are very few who have a plan prior to meeting someone, have an expectation time table after meeting them, and have a realistic picture for themselves to go by. I believe that each one of these steps are essential in feeling fulfilled in relationships. When time is not taken to create and execute a plan, a sub plan is formed and subsequently it just seems to destroy other people's plan.

I have read many books and listen to many "relationship gurus" who have had their own spin on how a relationship should go and transpire. I am not knocking their method. I believe they have their place but I believe the answers that we seek may be hidden in plain sight. These answers are within us and all around us. *STITCHES #1 - Everything you have ever experienced has happen for one of two reasons, either to help prepare you for something later in life you would face or to two, so you could help someone else who will go through something similar.* Yes, this means I'm saying that the relationship that you were head over heels in that ended tragically and all but broke your heart in a million pieces is but another step on the ladder to your successful relationship. Every relationship that materialized into something other than what we originally thought or planned actually was predestined. This concept should also raise several questions. What am I supposed to be getting out of it? Where do the lessons end and the real test begin? How do I graduate? While you are contemplating these questions, allow me to ask another. If the relationships in our lives were all on purpose, and every experience is but for one of two reasons, then does this mean that we know someone in our life that has been through what we are going through and they are just waiting to hear us ask or share what we are going through to give them the opening to share their life? While that may be deep, try this one; is there really such a thing a "soul mate" if there are billions of people on this planet and we are all stretched across the globe? The answer is simple. No, there is not such a thing "a soul mate". You have the potential to connect with dozens of people in your lifetime.

These answers are within us and all around us. There are three types of people that we envision when asked to describe the person we want to be with. They are the ideal partner, the realistic partner, and the settled for partner.

IDEAL PARTNER

If you think back to when you first started developing notions of what you found attractive, you created a mental picture of what the person you see yourself being with has to look like. This person is what I would call your "Ideal Partner". This person may have all the Hollywood style and swag or the glamour of your favorite Diva. When you close your eyes you see the likes of Denzel Washington or Channing Tatum. Men may see Kirby Griffin or Sofia Vergara. We dream that they would come bearing lots of money, be willing to obey our every command or wait on us hand and foot. Oh and don't forget that we are quick to say that they must just love us and do such indescribable sexual activities it can only be described outside of PG-13 status. The listing could go on forever and the fantasies over people that you only know from television, movie screens, and magazines could easily keep you hoping for something that is not impossible but in so many cases so farfetched that one might as well call it just that, impossible. The problem with our Ideal Partner is they lack all of the qualities that we look for past the initial request. Because they are based on the outside view of someone we see that we do not even know they lack all the characteristics that we need. Sure, if we were to link up with any of our fantasies, we might think we are in heaven for a while but just like new jewelry over time, the initial glamour will fade and the sparkle will eventually no longer shine in a light that draws other people's attention.

REALISTIC PARTNER

Then, just as life would have it, we don't necessarily grow out of our childhood fallacies but we start experimenting with what we believe is the next best thing to our Ideal Partner, and that is the Realistic Partner. This person is someone who has seemed to emerge from the dust of us waiting for our Ideal Partner to come along. As time passes and the reality that our knight in shining armor does not even know we exist, we start to give those around us with like characteristics of our Ideal Partner a chance. The problem with this partner is they do not pose the completed traits of the Ideal Partner so our expectations are doomed for disappointment. Our fuse is short because we soon find our lives filled with compromise. Because most of the traits that brought us to this partner were based on inexperience, we end up wandering aimlessly it seems. This is, however, how we get experience. I remember hearing about studies done not long ago about college graduates who were having problems finding jobs in the fields where their schooling had come because they lacked real world experience. I believe we should expect this same manner of expectation from relationships. Just like a job, it takes having a crappy job where your boss does not appreciate you to appreciate a good job when it comes along. It does not mean that when you get a good job, that you stop looking to advance but to always keep the door open so if there comes a time where there is no longer room for growth within the organization, you are not so engulfed that you cannot separate yourself when you need to.

Relationships work the same. The issue with the Realistic Partner is that we are forced to learn to deal with their shortcomings and most of the time they seem like tremendous ones. We take from Realistic Partnerships all of the negativity and add it to our relationship resume under experiences. I use to be a hiring manager at one of my former employments and I always found it interesting when I looked at work history. It was almost like credit. Too much gives off just as bad a signal as too little. Most people prefer a partner that they can show a new few tricks to but not someone with little to no experience. I believe these categories of people are the news most people get caught up on. The Realistic Partner is just someone to show you the ropes but all too often people stay involved with them past what they should.

SETTLE FOR PARTNER

Then there is the partner that people who, out of pure exhaustion, just decide they will deal with. They are normally someone that they never envisioned themselves with originally but after experiencing numerous unsuccessful relationships, either first hand or second, they dial back their expectations and accept what they tell themselves is the best they can get. When a person has never been in or around a successful relationship than their vision of what a positive relationship is supposed to look is obscured. They watch their mom settle for being used as an occasional punching bag or a father who cheats and claims it is as a result of loving his wife but not wanting to leave her. There are many levels of which people settle. When asking people who have admitted to settling, the most common responses were I just got tired of trying and they really are not that bad when you do not focus on their negative parts.

This is as a result of being taught to swallow their feelings and just keep going. There is a generation of fathers who in teaching their daughters to be independent and tough, have raised a breed who is emotionally detached from their feelings. When things do not go the way they envisioned, they do not know how to handle it. They are extremely hard on themselves. This derives from never being allowed to work through their own feelings for so long that after some time they concludes that everything is their fault.

Chapter 11

Baggage

The problem with most relationships is not the baggage that people knowingly bring into them, it is with the baggage that they have, know they have but act like it is not there. Now let's be honest. We all have baggage. Baggage is what we pick up from life's experiences that affect how we react to things, how we deal with people, and how we carry ourselves. All baggage is not bad baggage. For instance, it is only after you deal with someone who is independent that you determine if moving forward, you want someone else who is also independent or if you would rather have someone who just has independency. Either way, the baggage we carry from situation to situation affects us differently.

Ideally when we met someone we would like for their baggage to be displayed and scanned as it would be going through check in at an airport. First giving them an opportunity to dispose of anything that would be hazardous to anyone else around and then going through a thermo scan. The problem with baggage does not come when we are dealing with someone who is upfront with baggage that is not necessarily healthy but rather when things pop up that they claim to know nothing about. On my last trip to the airport, I remember hearing several announcements about baggage not being left unattended or taking packages from people that you do not know. We should treat the people we deal with every day with the same level of security and caution. Until we know what at least pops up during their initial scan, we should not pursue them past the outer lobby of our life. In other words, they should remain associates. They should not get VIP treatment or otherwise they may feel and act like they are entitled to more than they are. Then you will feel guilty and try and fast track them to the exclusive area prematurely. To catch a plane now, they tell you to be at the airport at least two hours before your flight so you can go through all of the proper checks and still make your flight on time. We should treat everyone we meet with the same expectation. If they are not willing to show up early, stand in a line or two for a few minutes, and undergo pre checks, then they may as well be labeled as a terrorist and should be treated hostile. I mean let's face it, what is the point of blood, sweat, and tears if you are not going to use the lessons it has taught you to better yourself. Would you knowingly let a terrorist come on a plane that you are boarding? Of course not! Then why do we let people in our lives without proper clearance. You need to know something about the people you deal with. Where they are from? Who have they been with? Who they people are? Have they picked up any habits, I mean packages, from strangers along the way?

Even after going through baggage check, people still can have extra stuff that can threaten your life. An example of this is insecurities. Let us say you have met this guy and he seems to have it pretty much together. He is a dream come true. You open up and allow him to board your life. Once in the air you realize he has tendencies. He always wants to know about the names of people from a previous manifest. He also asked repeatedly about current passengers who are just temporary passengers until the next stop or two. You understand his concerns but point out that none of these issues surfaced or questions were asked during initial boarding. You pacify him by giving him everything it seems that he would need but nothing is helping. He wants to dig deeper and ask more questions. This is a classic example of what I call "unauthorized baggage". Unauthorized baggage can have you off balance with very little to no clue as to why. When a partner is overly aggressive or possessive, it can weigh you down to the point where you are ready to start throwing things off. When nothing you do seems to be working, you will start eliminating things that are actually in your life to help you; like fuel, food or even extra oxygen (friends who give you life). Again, those closest to you will give you warning signs when this happens. Your body will also be a good sign of indicators. Do not ignore the signs. Pay attention, life has a way of getting your attention. If you are not careful you will find yourself starting to become distant with friends and even point the figure at others as the reason to why things are the way they are.

So how do you protect yourself? How do you protect others from what you may unknowingly offload onto them? The answer is simple but difficult. Most people know the answers that they seek; they just do not want to face them. To protect yourself, develop a system of how you deal with new people and reevaluate the ones in your life. Open up the lines of communication. You have to stop being afraid that your openness or inquisitive desire will draw people away from you. What is more important to you, hurting someone's feelings or being hurt after realizing you have wasted your time? I met someone once who I must admit first came across as brass. She was very short with guys that she met. She told them how she felt and what she was looking for. If they were not it, she told them almost immediately. I asked why she was so abrupt. I even asked if she even realized that she might have passed up some really good men. She told me yes, she was very aware of the possible consequences of her actions. The issue is she was fine with passing up a couple good men because she did not want just a good man, she wanted an exceptional one. Talking with her one day, she told me that she is looking for someone who can handle what she brings to the table and can meet eighty percent of her expectations. She said the problem with most people is that they only look for someone who has seemingly fifty percent of the qualities that they are looking for. Unfortunately they typically only end up with someone with thirty to thirty-five percent of it and after putting in time they realize just how much they are missing. They settle only to start looking elsewhere or being miserable years down the line. She said that will not be her. If they cannot meet at least eighty percent of her expectations then they can stay where they are. The baggage that they knowingly will have with them will cause a depreciation value of approximately fifteen to twenty percent. This will still leave them with over fifty percent of the qualities I am looking for and if the cards are played correctly, it will increase in value by at least ten to fifteen percent due to natural progression. Her argument sound convincing and I believe we all could take something from her example. Today, she is married with kids and living quite nicely. She often tells me that her relationship is not perfect but no relationship is. The time she put in at the beginning was worth the reward now. She had only dated and been with a hand full of guys and they were all worth the return investment. I asked her about baggage and how she dealt with it. Her response stunned me again. She said baggage is like faith. We all have a little but the only thing that counts is what we do with it. People do not care if you have issues. They have their own. They only care about how you are going to handle your business. Are you going to get bent out of shape? Are you going to let it ruin your life or are you going to let it just be another facet of displaying your abilities to manage your life? When you meet someone, you have baggage and you have to prepare them for dealing with your life. In doing this, you should first prioritize your baggage by the most life altering. Put yourself in the shoes of your potential or present partner. What would you want to know? What would be deal breakers for you? If you have a psycho ex or "baby momma drama", get your life in order before bringing someone else into that foolishness. Too often people try and cover up baggage by adding other "stuff" into their life. It only hurts things. Baggage is like a rash, you can cover it up but if you do not address it, it will only make things worse, festering under the covering. The best solution to solve your issues is what my mom told me once right after I had gotten out of a serious relationship, you need to spend time by yourself. You have to allow yourself time to get a person out of your system. If you have ever found yourself holding your present partner responsible for things that they had not even done but you have strong reservations about, chances are, you are not over something. Now I know nobody wants to be told that they are not over their ex but the truth is, most people suffer from post-traumatic stress from previous relationships. If gone untreated, they can make your present relationship go through unnecessary mayhem.

This does require a degree of maturity. You have to be mature enough to admit when you realize an unauthorized baggage has emerged. Stop waiting to gauge how your present partner will react. We have to become more proactive instead of reactive. If you have found yourself no longer feeling the same way you did earlier in the relationship or marriage, tell them. Do not delay. Time will only make things worse. Your partner learns your habits and even if you are trying not to show them, they will show and tell. They will show through your actions and tell from your responses to things. For example, you are dating this girl and things are going well but you start noticing that you are irritable with her regarding other guy friends she has. At this point there are several factors and issues which need to be address. First, the person with the issue needs to recognize that they are indeed having an issue; weather it is warranted or not, meaning with proper cause. At this point, the other party has a responsibility. Their answer should not be that it is just their issue and they need to deal with it. It is their issue and they do have the right to address it but you must have the understanding that them bringing it to you is them starting to address the issue. You have to be understanding and make noticeable attempts to help them address their issue. If it is insecurities, then reassuring them in those areas will go a long way. This is more than just saying trust me or it is not what you think. Again, put yourself in their shoes. Have standards but be understanding. Have the standards so you are not compromising or just going along with anything but have the type of understanding where you can relate to your partner is facing and or going through.

Chapter 12

Get Over Them

We have all had them, you know, the ones we seem to never be able to forget. The ones we compare everyone we meet to. The ones we just cannot put out of our minds. We all know that ex's are in our past for a reason and if you heard like me from the old folks, "they are in our past for reason so leave them there." We have all heard this before but what about when you can't?

A friend asked me recently about an ex of hers and why it seemed that she could not put him out of her mind and system. She had tried everything it seemed. She went to church and "laid" it on the altar; asking God to help her move on. She tried cutting off all lines of communication and even dating other guys. Just to help push herself past him. At the end of it all she still found herself waking up in the middle of the night reaching for him and wondering if she was the only one with these feelings. None of the other guys seemed to pan out because for some reason she could never develop the level of feelings and emotions for them like they expressed toward her. The more she rationalized the situation, the more she found herself even more confused and distorted. He had moved on and she could not seem to. She was even more puzzled about her feelings when they were still there and he had gotten married. Now, we know it is wrong to covet another man or woman's spouse but what if they were in your soul before they married them? The bottom line is that this type of scenario happens all the time. So what does it take to move on with our lives? As I pose this question, think of what it would take for you to be happy. The reason many of us cannot move past someone in our past is because we choose not to move past our past. I say choose not to because it is indeed a choice. We would rather hold on to reminisces than take from the experience of being with the person and move on with our lives. Every person we are involved with, whether we are willing to admit it or not, are meant to teach us something. It is from those lessons that we find the strength to close a chapter in our lives and move on to what is next for us. This sounds simple but I am very aware that it is far from easy. The initial choices we make are easy; dealing with the positive and negative consequences as well as the process that follows are the difficult part. *STITCHES # 105- The choice is simple, in the process lies the challenge.*

What would you do if you found out the one person in your life who claimed to be your friend through thick and thin and to always have your back was nothing more than a leech? There are two kinds of friends in this world, those who come to add to your life and those that come to take from it, but what do you do at that moment when the last one you thought was on your side for the long haul ended up just like so many others with ulterior motives?

These are the issues. The real ones you and I face every day. We were all told as kids that we cannot make it through this world alone. We were designed to have connections with other people. Those "other people" often become the most influential factors in our lives. They help navigate our decision making in everything from fashion taste to the approval of a significant other and who we choose as friends play such an integral part that how we choose them is crucial. But how do you determine these people and how do they pertain to learning one's self.

Well the second part of that is easy to answer but the first, not so much. The concept of learning yourself is important to determining who you choose as friends because understanding who you are will help you make better decisions about those you choose to associate with. In a way, choosing your friends are a prelim to determining who your significant other will be because it gives you the character practice which is essential. Just think have you ever met someone who had friends that just did not seem to match with their personality. I am not talking about the friends that argue all the time but the ones that make you sit back and wonder why are they or are we friends.

To move past someone, we need to examine and meditate on what we were supposed to take from being with them. Think past the surface level good or bad times, the moments that took your breath away or the feelings which make you cringe every time you think of them. We learn something from every experience we witness. We are witnesses to experiences all the time but we are only first-hand witnesses to things where we were the star actors. Our mindset has to change from just being a primary or secondary witness but to being a subject matter expert witness. Often in court cases, lawyers call first hand witnesses, then rebuttal or second hand witnesses but neither take the place of having a subject matter expert to call. The regular witnesses cannot give you an unbiased account of what has happen but a subject matter expert looks at all the evidence and bases its testimony on an outside view looking into the situation.

This is how you must examine your previous relationships. Ask yourself not just about the surface level evidence but the meaning behind the results. When you do this, you will find that what you seek and need to move on has been in plain sight but you just could not see it. To move past your past, reexamine your plans to move forward and reevaluate your expectations of what you expect out of a partner. This is a key but not to the extent that you base what you are looking for solely on the traits that were either present or absent from the previous relationship. If you focus on finding someone just like or completely opposite of your previous relationship, you will more than likely end up with a "repeat offender". A repeat offender is when you search for someone based on a previous partner and end up creating a copycat relationship. This is why many people find themselves repetitively dating people that cheat on them. This is also very common among victims of domestic abuse who end up in a cycle of the same types of partners.

It's not our fault but we are our worse enemy. After every relationship, there should be a time of reflection and self examination. When I was separated from my first wife, my mother told me that I should not go running and jumping into another relationship. I needed time to get my past partner out of my system. I heard her but chose not to listen, at least not initially. I met this lady who was as I would like to describe as "smokin". She was everything opposite of my ex and in my sight, everything I was looking for. The problem came several weeks into the relationship when I started taking things out on her that she had nothing to do with. It is not fair to bring anyone into your life when you have not taken the time to get over your past. I remember starting arguments and not even knowing why I started them. I remember being upset and making a big deal out of the simplest, most innocent things. There was this one time when her car was broken down and I was taking her back and forth to work; I got all upset and bent out of shape because I told myself she was using me for a ride to and from work; when in fact, I was the one who volunteered to help her out while her car was being worked on in the first place. I also remember fussing about something relating to how my kids should have been taken care of and I "blew a gasket" because she did or did not do something. I recall her even sitting me down and explaining that they were not her kids to begin with but because she chose to be with me, she not only excepted them also but she was trying her best with them, since she did not have children of her own. Now I am sure that you are reading this and saying that I am such an awful person but this happens in relationships all the time. I eventually pushed her completely away; severely hurting her and she never even understood why. This is what happens when you do not allow the natural healing process of moving past being in a relationship with someone to take place. You cannot speed up the process. You have to allow it to take its natural course. This is what I call stitches. We often try and put a bandage cure on a wound that really needed stitches. The solutions to getting over someone is not to just jump in another relationship. This is just putting on a band-aid. We have wounds when we leave relationships. We need time to ourselves to let them begin to heal. We often meet people before our wounds are completely healed but at that point they are no longer in need of stitches but just time. This time period varies from person to person and situation to situation. Getting over someone is never easy. It is a challenge. We all have shortcomings and need time to work on us. Only you know the right amount of time you need to yourself. Only you know when you are ready to introduce yourself to the world and begin the process all over again. *STITCHES #107- It is not fair to bring anyone into your life when you have not taken the time to get over your past.*

So the answer to this question of whether we will ever get a person completely out of our system is simple also. No. The whole idea of the person being seemingly stuck in our minds is just as a constant reminder of the lessons learned from those experiences. They are meant to help us make better decisions going forward. Treasure them. Memories are a dime a dozen and one of life's greatest gifts.

Chapter 13

Trying is Not the Same as Giving It Your All

How many of us would be honest enough with, if no one else, ourselves, and say that we honestly don't give all that we can to our efforts? Truthfully, we run around complaining about what our partner does not do and use as the excuse that we trying. I heard recently that the word trying is a synonym for acceptable failure. In other words it is our way of preparing others for when we fail. If this indeed is the case, then why do we even go through the motions? You know what? Don't answer that, allow me. Deep down we do not want to succeed. If our relationships were to be successful then we would have little to talk about in our minds. Not in the sense that it would not be worth bragging on but because we would then be considered out of the norm and it is no longer socially acceptable to be different in a positive way. Everybody wants to fit in. Now before you go rolling your eyes and saying I am wrong for this, check my references......you! How many times have you taken your single girlfriend's advice that seemed to have all the right answers but they are single themselves? How about the numerous times you have had a gut feeling but ignored it because it would have required you to act differently from your norm? If this sounds like you then you have short changed yourself. You have been living a life with a false sense of expectations. I mean really what good are you doing hoping and wishing if you are sabotaging yourself at the same time? Over and over again life has shown us that if we take shortcuts or skip steps then we will fall short or end up with a false sense of accomplishment. We are willing to accept this principle everywhere else but in relationships or our everyday lives. How often have you heard yourself say that you have been trying? All the while saying let me prepare for when failure arrives.

DO WE SABOTAGE OURSELVES?

Do we really set ourselves up for failure? Yes, we do! All the time! We do the equivalence of getting into a car without a destination or goal. It is like driving aimlessly without a goal or plan. It does not make much sense but neither does going into a relationship and saying "we will just see where things go." How often have you meet someone or had friends who claim to be single and just wanted or had "friends"? They said it is just so much more convenient; a "relationship without all the strings," they claim. But is it really less of a headache or do we just try to psych ourselves out? The truth is we need to stop trying to cut corners. We only end up having to go back and repeat experiences. You cannot cut corners when it comes to getting to know someone and what you expect from them. The problem is we have so much hurt from previous experiences that we harbor those feeling well past the experience. There is a slim line between learning the lesson from an experience and letting an experience cause you to be afraid of new experiences. I remember a friend telling me that they were done with relationships all together. Their partner had done something which caused them to question whether they could trust or move forward with them. This is not anything new. We all have been in this position. We think we know the person we are with and give them the benefit of the doubt until they do something dramatic and we are forced to face the obvious. The signs were always there, we just purposely at first and eventually unknowingly ignore them. The way habits work is we force ourselves to do things at first but after a while we do not even realize we are doing it. Have you ever stopped and asked yourself if you had put on deodorant? You had gotten so use to going through the motions, you honestly do not remember if you did it. The same concept applies to the things we except from our partner in relationships. What at first seemed hard to swallow and except, begins to feel like normal. For instance, a man who abuses his woman may first start off as just demeaning words, then a shove or snatching something from her. Most times woman except it because they are designed to want to please their partner. They want to serve them. They are so use to men claiming they are "nagging" when they are expressing their beliefs and opinions. The issue is this, so women pay attention, a man respects what is firm and consistent. When you go to a man with your expressions or opinions, state them firmly and move on. You do not have to dwell on what is a standard for you. If you do not except a man who does not make his own money, tell him and make him come up to the standard. If he does not come up to your standard, move on. He would do the same to you. We often mess over ourselves by accepting what we know good and well we are not good with putting up with later. Yet and still, we stick around and say they will change. News flash, public service announcement, YOUR PARTNER will not change just because you want them to. The way they are when you met them is pretty much how they are going to be down the road. Stop lying to yourself and thinking if you do more and try not to cause confusion, things will go the way you envision. Life nor men, women, or children work that way. All you can do is state your expectations and desires, then determine before you get emotionally connected if they are going to adjust to you or if you are going to adjust to them.

The older I get, the more I understand that the valuable thing in life is my time. Not too long ago I was talking to a friend's son about video games. He expressed his deep belief that after spending hours a day at school he felt he should be allowed to know someone and what you expect from them. The problem is we have so much hurt from previous experiences that we harbor those feeling well past the experience. There is a slim line between learning the lesson from an experience and letting an experience cause you to be afraid of new experiences. I remember a friend telling me that they were done with relationships all together. Their partner had done something which caused them to question whether they could trust or move forward with them. This is not anything new. We all have been in this position. We think we know the person we are with and give them the benefit of the doubt until they do something dramatic and we are forced to face the obvious. The signs were always there, we just purposely at first and eventually unknowingly ignore them. The way habits work is we force ourselves to do things at first but after a while we do not even realize we are doing it. Have you ever stopped and asked yourself if you had put on deodorant? You had gotten so use to going through the motions, you honestly do not remember if you did it. The same concept applies to the things we except from our partner in relationships. What at first seemed hard to swallow and except, begins to feel like normal. For instance, a man who abuses his woman may first start off as just demeaning words, then a shove or snatching something from her. Most times woman except it because they are designed to want to please their partner. They want to serve them. They are so use to men claiming they are "nagging" when they are expressing their beliefs and opinions. The issue is this, so women pay attention, a man respects what is firm and consistent. When you go to a man with your expressions or opinions, state them firmly and move on. You do not have to dwell on what is a standard for you. If you do not except a man who does not make his own money, tell him and make him come up to the standard. If he does not come up to your standard, move on. He would do the same to you. We often mess over ourselves by accepting what we know good and well we are not good with putting up with later. Yet and still, we stick around and say they will change. News flash, public service announcement, YOUR PARTNER will not change just because you want them to. The way they are when you met them is pretty much how they are going to be down the road. Stop lying to yourself and thinking if you do more and try not to cause confusion, things will go the way you envision. Life nor men, women, or children work that way. All you can do is state your expectations and desires, then determine before you get emotionally connected if they are going to adjust to you or if you are going to adjust to them.

The older I get, the more I understand that the valuable thing in life is my time. Not too long ago I was talking to a friend's son about video games. He expressed his deep belief that after spending hours a day at school he felt he should be allowed to forget all his worries and cares and become engulfed in fantasy worlds frequently and with very little to no interruption. Instead of telling him he was wrong and how much I thoroughly disagreed with his thought process, I asked him one question, "Ultimately, what benefit does it bring to your life?" I know that some would say that my line of questioning was too deep for an eighth grader but this is the same young man who said he had done his research and found that colleges only look as far back as your ninth grade year when they are looking at grades and he figured he had a little while longer to "goof off". My response to him and to you who are serious about your future is that you have to go pass the minimum standards. You have to determine what things are assets bringing substance to your life and what are liabilities bringing temporary, if any, value to you. In the case of the student I was talking to, I encouraged him to examine his life and what things are bring him potential benefits. I shared with him how I enjoy occasional game play myself but I make a point to remind myself that I cannot afford to get lost in something that will not bring benefits to my life. Many people in relationships look for releases and we all should have them but we have to remember that releases are temporary and we cannot get caught up in something that was only meant to be around for a moment. Otherwise, we could wake up and so much of our present thought process is now everyone else's past.

Chapter 14

Don't Quit Short

We often find ourselves in what seems like the fight of our lives. We go from one life crisis to the next. The only thing worse is when the crises compound and seem to come at us all at once. We feel like the walls are falling down and we cannot get a break or do anything right. We have to remember that despite the appearances, it is darkest before the break of day. Life gives us clues and signs but we just have to know what to look at. The very things that seem to be disheartening are the previews of what is to come. They may not look like what we would like or how we envisioned them but it all has to do with preparing us for what is next in our lives. If you look back on your life or ask someone in their late thirties or older to look back over their life, they would tell you that some of the things they thought brought them the greatest joys actually turned out to be shadows of sorrow. They would say some experiences that were believed to just have to be endured because they were the least enjoyed brought the greatest rewards. What I am trying to say is, life does not work on our timeline or schedule. When we were young, we were told that the sky is the limit and we could be anything we wanted to be when we grew up. We pressed forward with this notion and belief only to find out that our beliefs were short lived when reality set in. This is where most of us are today. Stuck in that place after realizing our dreams have shadows and our goals have nightmares. In a place where we no longer want to try because of lost hope. According to how we see it, life has dealt us such a blow that we do not even know where to start now. I am reminded of a story in which an army was told to march around the gates of a city once every day for seven days. The key was that the soldiers did not know when or how many days or times they would march around the gates. Every day that they went out was under the umbrella of that day being the one where their opportunity would come and they would go into battle. If you could imagine one of the soldiers coming home after the first day and his wife, who kissed her husband off goodbye many times before not knowing if it would be her last being able to do so, asking him how the day went and how successful he was in the battle. He, more than likely unsure of her next response, said hi we just scoped out the city and came home.

The next day he did the same and came home to an awaiting wife who was excited to see him and anxious to exchange stories of how the day had gone. His story was the same for several days, six to be exact. I am pretty sure after a couple days the wife's response as he came back home kind of changed. She may have stopped asking him altogether about what happened, seemed less interested, or even began using sarcasm or criticism in regards to how the battle was being handled. Can't you hear her telling him that he would have gotten more done had he just stayed at the house with her? Then at least, he could have helped out around the house. On the seventh day, after completing the final patrol just as the previous six days, the leader of the army turned and instructed the army to holler with a loud and thunderous voice. When they did, the walls of the city fell and they were able to go in and win the fight. The issue with so many of us is that we get stalled in the days leading up to the fight. We can even be promised the victory if we would just stick around for the fight but we get overwhelmed with preparation. You have to come to the understanding that there is a preparation period to prepare you for what is next in your life. In college, I had some classes I could not take until after I took some other class or classes. They were called prerequisite. Although they might not have made sense at the time, they were necessary because the class you were really interested in, or needed, started from where the prerequisite class left off. In other words, we only go through things for one of two reasons; one to prepare us for something later in life that we will face. And for two, so we can assist someone else as they face it. So, despite things appearing to be compound, we have to remember that it is all a set up. We just have to go through the process.

Knowing that it is a process does not make it any less daunting or easier. It does give us hope though. We have to look at it through the lenses of a task not yet completed. Not as failure or even incomplete. I am sure the first couple days when the soldier came home, he felt a little wired telling his friends and family, who looked up to him so much, that they were still "just spying out the land" and that they were working on their skill set. But I would guess that after about the third or fourth day, patience got short and tempers probably began to flare. It got hard to suit up in full gear and convince yourself that they might actually fight that day. It was a mental battle they had to push through. It is one thing to be questioned or looked at kind of cross eyed or funny when other people begin doubting you but to encourage yourself when you start doubting yourself, that is a whole different challenge in and of itself. By day four or five, they probably started looking at themselves crossed eyed and wondering what they were doing. You may be in your day five or six right now. Things seem to be headed in a downward swirl and nothing you do to make it better is working. I want to encourage you to stay the path. Keep focused. Make sure everything you are doing is lining up with getting you to your goal.

For instance, a few months back I began the serious challenge of losing weight and changing my lifestyle for one of a healthier pattern. The reason why I say it like this is because a lot of people claim to want to do better and say they will make changes in their lives. They go on diets, starve themselves, and spend hundreds of dollars in an attempt to quickly fix what they see as something wrong with them. Unfortunately, it is not that simple. What took years to create cannot just be undone with a pill or a short term change in eating habits. I have nothing against dieting, but most folks who diet end up falling off the wagon and gaining more weight than they had before they got started. The key is to make small changes and be consistent with it. *STITCHES #190 - Stick to change until you see change*. When I started going to the gym and working the plan which I created, I did not see results initially. I would go and embarrassingly enough, I would hide behind baggy clothes and skip the exercises that I knew I did not look good doing. Although, I was in the place I knew was designed for me to train and get stronger, I was afraid to show weakness, even to myself. We struggle with what I call "self-shadow". It is always there, reminding us of our other us, the stronger, smarter, more confident side of us. The stitch for this wound is consistently perfect practice. Growing up, we were often fed one of life's most inaccurate beliefs: Practice makes perfect. This could not be farther from the truth. Practice alone does not make perfect. If a person is practicing wrong, they are no closer to being perfect than someone who is not practicing at all. They are wasting time. If you learn wrong, you have to unlearn bad habits and learn new correct ones. So, the only way that practice can make perfect is if you practice perfectly. You must practice correctly until you practice perfectly, then you continue to practice perfectly so when it is time to perform, you will do it perfectly as well.

When I first started going to the gym, I did not see the results of my work; not immediately, not even for a while but I had to just keep working my plan. If you are working a plan right now, first check to see if the end result is where you truly want to go and what you want to do. The plan I had fifteen to twenty years ago is not the same plan I have today. You are allowed to change it. If it is not working for you or you have realized that you want something different now, then make adjustments.

Next, check the guide for getting to your goal or goals. In other words, check your map. Make sure it is accurate and does not get you there too soon or take too long. If you try and cut too many corners, it can lead to derailment or setbacks. If you take too long, you can easily get side tracked and lose sight of your intended destination. Along the way, make sure you have rest stops and fueling stations. The rest stops will allow you to refocus, rejuvenate, and check your status. Although, life does not give us signals or clues on some things such as sickness, death, or redirecting, we can be prepared. After all, we all know that it is afforded to every man (or woman) to live and to die, sickness is a part of life, and things happen which are beyond our control. We just have to stay focused on the road and the journey ahead and not be sidelined by flat tires along the way. We also need gas stations, they are where we refuel. We get our refuel met in a number of ways. Physically, we have to take care of our bodies. We need to eat healthy, exercise regularly, fuel our emotional side as well as our spiritual being. Our emotional refueling comes from the relationships we have. Positive or negative, they both serve as fuel. I remember my mechanic told me he was putting some dye in some lines in my engine in order to determine where I might have a leak. Although, the car was never designed for dye, it may be necessary from time to time to flush out inhibitors or bring to the surface to identify the problems. They all serve their purpose. Once you know why they are in your life, it will allow you to address them accordingly. The other part of the refueling is on a spiritual level. Regardless of what you believe in, your spirit is filled by something. As humans we are designed with a need for affirmation. Whatever we believe in, we look to be encouraged and reaffirmed in it. From time to time on your journey, spiritual refueling is essential to keep your life in balance and remember the purpose for your journey.

The next stitch is checking for accuracy. Many would say this goes without saying but I beg to differ. Too often, people feel they have a flawless plan but they cannot understand why things are not working as they thought. It is because there is an error in the program. When I was a freshman in college, I thought I wanted to be a computer science major. This was until I took my first C++ class. I learned very quickly how easy it was to make mistakes and not have anything work. I remember building a program, thinking it was the "bomb" until my professor came around and asked me to run it. When I did, it failed horribly. I remember him saying, "There may be something on the back end which is causing the error. Go back and check for accuracy." We often do not realize we have done wrong until we get an error code. We have two choices then; we can sit and stare at our failure or go back and find what went wrong, make some adjustments, and then work our plan again with the adjustments.

The next stitch that needs to be checked is to make sure faith is not the only driving force but also fortitude. Faith believes something can happen or that you can do something but fortitude is seeing it through. A lot of people say they are going to write a book, one day. If you talk to them they will convince you that they can do it and you may very well walk away with high aspirations but if they do not poses the fortitude to make it happen then their faith is coupled with only potential. I was in a relationship once where I had all the faith in the world in my partner. I believed she could conquer Mount Everest if she just put forth the effort. I spent years trying to get her there. I remember being asked several times by several people what it was that it saw in her. I never could answer. It was not until we had gone our separate ways that I finally figured out what it was. I was drawn to her potential. All the signs were there and all the elements appeared to be in place for her to reach what I had seen in my mind her achieving. The only problem was it was what I envisioned for her and not what she envisioned for herself. It was also no fortitude. Potential is what you could be or what you could become. Fortitude is the drive, determination and will to get you to your goal. *STITCHES #111 - We all possess faith, we see potential, but we have to be taught fortitude.* The bottom line is we have to see our plans through. We just cannot get stuck in the process. We cannot sell ourselves short and stop on the sixth day. Our breakthrough could be just around the bend. The ironic part about the story of the soldiers is that they never knew when the day they would actually have to fight would come. So they had to treat every day like it was the day. They did not have time to worry about if it was just another day to go about a routine. They had to always be ready and so do we. How do we always be ready? I'm so glad you asked; it's simple. We have to treat every day like it could be the day. We have to treat every day like the breakthrough, miracle, or outcome which we desperately need could and will come today. Kiss that family member as though it might be the last one you will have together. Do your job as if your promotion is counting on it. Spend time with that parent as if you will not get another chance to. Make that decision as if your life depended on it, because it just might. Why, because life gives us no clue of what destiny has in store for us.

Chapter 15

Rain

Have you ever thought about rain? Is it not amazing how the very concept of rain can be interpreted differently for several people? I'm at home, sitting in my favorite chair relaxing after a busy morning of errands, I look out the screen door and notice the rain coming down rather profusely. I think about how soothing it is to listen to and how I can just see myself taking a nap, while listening to it in the background. I also think about how inconvenient it seemed not too long ago, when I had to drive home in it then get out of my car and go through it to get into the house. At that moment, it was so soothing and calming and I wanted to do a number of things but none of them were rest. Then lastly, I thought about what it was like when I used to go out and play or work in the rain. When I could not escape it and I was fine with that. This same thought process can be thought of when we think of the troubles in relationships we experience. Rain is natural and we all can probably agree necessary. Trials are the same way. If we had the choice of whether to be caught up in them we would more than likely choose the latter. We would rather avoid all manners of uncomfortable circumstances as we can because we only want to deal with them when we are forced to. Watching other people go through rain is often entertaining. Although, we know they refine our character and they must come, it does not change how we feel. The first step towards improving the outcome after the rain is to understand it. Where does rain come from? Rain comes from clouds. Where do the clouds reside? Clouds reside in the sky. Where does rain fall? Rain falls to the ground. What does it do to the vegetation below? It helps it to grow. Where does it grow? Vegetation grows up toward the sky. Okay, I know you are saying that sounded a little elementary but sometimes things need to be broken down in what I call "blue's clues style". In the same way clouds reside in the sky and share their contents with the variables below, we must start learning our place. I often hear people reference taking the "high road" but I pose the argument and question, "should not that be where you reside always?"

Have you ever heard of clouds coming to the ground and addressing the variables below on what it shares with them? Do not answer; I got this one for you. No, they do not. They remain in their position. They calculate their position and timing as to where and when to share their outpour. Then, almost as on cue, they changed the entire outlook of the variables they encounter. By now you should be noticing the relations with my analogy.

Rain is going to come. Stop harping on when and where it comes from. It is nice to know but there is very little that you can do about it coming other than prepare for how to handle it. Some rain is light and you can continue your day as if it does not really change that much while other rains will change your plans altogether. Either way, stay in your space, learn your place, and prepare for when the rain comes.

Another factor to consider is that the clouds share its contents to bring the variables below up to its level. Vegetation grows upward toward where the clouds reside. This does not mean we walk around as if our heads are in the clouds and we are above everyone else around us but rather in a way to encourage others to come up to our level. This applies to every form of relationships. From the boss that seems to talk to you like you are incompetent, to the significant other who is apparently insecure and always questions every little thing you do, or even the petty gossip that your name seems to keep being brought up in and you have no clue how. *STITCHES #80 - When you know who you are and what level you reside on, you don't have to defend it to anyone else. Just reside.*

Chapter 16: Love is Work; Change is Necessary

Have you ever sat back and thought about how many single people talk about finding the love of their lives and married people or couples who have been together for what seems like eternity talk about how they wish they were either with someone else or just by themselves? Well this is because we all desire the prize until we have it for a while and realize it is not all that it originally cracked up to be. Here is a news flash - "love is work". We think that it comes naturally but it does not. We actually are just so focused on the prize at the beginning we do not realize all the time, effort, and work we put in to getting it. Then once we have it, things slow down for us. We are longer chasing the prize it rather just staring at the trophy.

It is like being in a competition for a prize but not realizing there is a prize after the goal. Instead of obtaining the prize and using it to move to the next one, we just sit and stare at that which we have already received. This is how we treat a number of our relationships. We work so hard to find someone compatible and then we just stop working. We expect things to just fall into place. Then when they do not, we view it as a failure but not for the reason of ignorance as we should. Yes, I said ignorance because if you do not understand love, then you are ignorant of how to use it properly. If you treat love like that trophy and put it on the shelf, over time it will collect dust and loose its luster. Next thing you know, you will be off to the next shiny and new attractive prize. There is hope. You can change your situation by changing your thought process. Be prepared to put in the work that comes along with love. Love is a verb, demonstrated by actions. If you are not doing something to illustrate your love, then you will find yourself "falling out of love".

Most of us are familiar with the age old analogy of the light bulb coming on for people. It is that moment when you realize something that either you should have known already because others around kept telling you or it just hits you. In other words, you have an epiphany. This is when change occurs. No one can pinpoint when this happens to people until after they see the effects of the change. The friend that you have told has been dating this loser of a guy, the middle age person who despite obvious intelligence never reached their potential, or the student who seemed to be in school forever, aimless searching but with no end seemingly in sight. Then, as if the flashlight of their life popped on, they change their stride.

So what can we do for these people in our lives? Unfortunately we cannot turn the light bulb on for the people we know who appear to desperately need an intervention. Until not too long ago, I did not realize the full gravity of the answer to this question myself. *STITCHES #94 - Change is reflective.* The good book refers to removing the plank out of your own eye before attempting to remove the speck out of someone else's. If we would just take the time to work on our shortcomings then people around us will see our change. That change will bring about one or two reflective changes. They will change things in their own life either positively or negatively. I noticed shortly after my wife started grad school, my thought process concerning my continued education changed. I started thinking about graduate and doctorate level education for myself. Was it because I did not want her to leave me behind or that I saw the change in her and it exposed me to the potential I had in myself. You never know the power that you have over other people when you harness what you have inside of yourself.

There are a number of motivators that bring about change in people. We may not know which one applies to a person or to ourselves until it happens but one thing we can be assured is that the change is reflective. The best way to open another person's eyes is to allow them to see you walking in a fresh view because your eyes are open. The next thing and just as critical is to not broadcast that your eyes are open and that they need to change. Change is a natural process that may be brought on by events or people but it still has to be accepted and executed. No one likes to be made to look foolish or put on blast just as much as no one wants to be emotionalized into change.

In an attempt to understand what factors caused change in people and how the changes differed, I interviewed a number of people. I have found that there are many factors. A lot of people have great intentions to change but it never happens. There are others who experience change but it does not last and others change for the duration. Like many others, this intrigued me. I was better able to understand these people and help determine which category fits. Better determine how to get in the place where you really want to be. The four factors that I have discovered which are necessary to bring about long term to permanent change all have to do with a personal sense of responsibility. These factors are change is by choice, one must have a desire to change, want to change, and be committed to change.

Change is a Choice

You have to realize that change cannot be brought about by you. You have to choose change. The world is filled with plenty of people who choose not to change despite seeing change all around them. I can remember my parents saying to stay off of social media and now they are my friends on several sites. Heraclitus, a Greek Philosopher, once said nothing endures but change. In other words there is nothing permanent but change. Nothing is permanent except change. The only constant is change. Heraclitus also spoke of everything flowing and how nothing stands still. We are all changing. Whether we except it or actively act in it, we are all a part of change. If you don't believe this just go outside and do nothing, just stand there. The day and time will still pass. The same concept applies if you choose not to change. The world may leave you behind while it changes. It took years for me to learn this lesson. I knew someone who had and has tons of potential. They have the capability to do several things and be successful in them but as a sense of choice, they decided they would rather choose to not be successful. Change occurred around them but they simply decided not to accept it. Eventually we all accept change; the question is whether it will be on our terms or others.

THE LIGHT BULB

They have the capability to do several things and be successful in them but as a sense of choice, they refuse to pursue any of the avenues. This is like so many people who have countless plans to be a success but they lack the depth to see those things become a reality. I spent years investing into this friend before finally realizing that I stopped evolving into what and where I wanted to go because I spent so much time pushing them. *STITCHES # 82 - We can see all the potential we want to in someone else but if it is not on their radar, then all it will ever be is what they could have become.* Either this can be because it is just your dream for them or because they do not desire for it to be so. In my case, my friend did not desire it to be their future. I hung around for years waiting and trying to persuade them to change. I came up for air one day long enough to see that I was losing myself and the things that make me who I was. The difficult part was I never understood the effects until after I separated myself from them. There lack of desire was infecting my character like a disease. I experienced years of stagnate growth because of the infection. I was hanging out with another friend who had known me for years one day and they asked me what was going on with me. I did not seem like the same person I once was. I could not answer no matter how hard I tried. I just knew I was not happy and that something had to change. The days just seem to blend in with each other and eventually I begin to think there no point of anything and the desires and dreams I once had could no longer happen so I did not push myself pass the least amount of work I had to do daily. My friend asked what caused me to lose my motivation but I could not answer. When your dream is drained from you like a disease, you cannot pinpoint when it left, you just know it is gone and often you do not even realize that until it has been gone for some time. My friend then gave me some advice that changed my direction. She told me to think back to the last time I remember having a sense of drive and motivation. As I thought back, it was some years back but it was before I allowed my motivation to be sucked up out of me. My friend then told me I have to want to get back there.

A WANT TO CHANGE

I could not go back in time and change the events which had transpired but I could change some things in my life. It is not enough to just have a desire to change. Plenty of people pose a desire or dreams. You have to make up in your mind that you are willing to do what it takes to see the change come to fruition. Some people argue there is no difference between desire and want but the differences are clearly displayed in the actions. One can have desire but lack the want but one cannot have want without desire. Desire is the vision of seeing yourself there and want is what it takes to get you from where you are to where you desire to be. The want is the driving force. This differs from person to person but is totally necessary to make a dream happen. You must be commitment to change. The lesson from the experience was you cannot invoke change over someone else unless they choose to except it; be careful and mindful of the people you have in your life who you have extended their season because they can very well start sucking the life out of you.

So why do we stay? What makes a man or a woman be that someone different? You know, outside the stereotype or unfortunately, the expected, the kind of person that others admire. When you see the happy couple going about their daily routine and you wonder if their love was always as fresh and alive or if they are really as in love as they appear? What makes a person decide to be all in or totally committed to their partner? I ventured to ask some couples what the key was and no one would or could give me just one answer. All of their responses steered around concepts that were endearing of their significant other. Although I am one of those people, I found myself not completely knowing why until recently. I, like so many, thought it was just so you can expect the same level of commitment from your spouse or because it was "in the vows". But let us be honest, people throw those two reasons out the window every day. So why then? What makes them step away from the circuit and shut down the simulator? Well the answer is both realistic and imaginable. People commit for the personal sense of wholeness. Now I know you are saying this cannot be it completely. It sounds the same thing as staying committed because your partner is. Well I disagree; every person who is committed may or may not have always been. What I mean by that is that some people stand on their personal morals and beliefs that they will not break vows and then later find the answers others come to learn all the same. The reason we stay committed is the big picture. I saw a movie about two men who enjoyed crashing weddings. I think most readers of books like this are familiar, but there was a part in the movie where one of the characters visited a funeral to pick up chicks; not saying I support that in any way. Anyways, as he was looking around at the family and friends who had gathered, he was drawn to the obvious widower who was weeping uncontrollably. In the movie, it was that moment where he realized that his lies, deceits, and shenanigans were feudal. This is the moment I am referring to; the moment when your world is different. The bird's singing seems pleasant. The air is clearer and it is as if someone has opened up a window to your used-to-be cloudy view and it all of a sudden now clear. Life as not a single event but a series of them that work together for the good of those willing to work and are patient.

This experience comes differently for us all. You must be mature enough to handle it, smart enough to recognize it and wise enough to walk in it. So what am I saying? I am saying that it is not rocket science but you do have to look for it. I have a favorite quote that my friends look at me funny whenever I say it. "It is math, not science." The solutions that we seek when it comes to happiness is not about being lucky or the use of the scientific method even, it is about seeing where you are at this stage in your life and utilizing the tools or assets available to you to determine where you are.

If you are tired of running into the same dead end type of people and you are tired of dating different kinds, with no difference in results, then it may just be time for you to stop looking. Yes, I said it, quit looking. When we try and force something that is just not our time to have, we just cause ourselves unnecessary frustrations. All in all we end up back at the drawing board all over again. I know I am not telling you something you have not heard before. So how about when are you going to apply the principles? Many of our issues are self-inflicted; simply because we do not take the time to evaluate our surroundings and situations and just run from one hopeless situation to the next. If your partner does not seem to treat you the way you ask them to or desire, what are you doing to change it? One of my personal favorite quotes is "different results comes from those willing to do things differently". With that said, what are you doing different to cause or initiate the change that you are expecting. Try paying a little more attention to your significant other in areas that are important to them and watch their reaction when they do not think you are looking. Now allow me to pause right here and give a word of caution. The person you are showing additional interest in can and will be able to tell if you are acting reluctant in your task. Do not think you can fake this and actually reap the benefits that someone who genuinely shows interest gets. Actually act it out. After all, the reason why you are with them is because you saw something in them that made you want to be with them more than anyone else. So often we stop working on being in each other's world once we get over the initial agreement. I urge you to continue to show interest, the real kind. After you have opened up the door of communication by showing interest in what they want or find.

Chapter 16

Why Do We Stay?

After you have opened up the door of communication by showing interest in what they want or find important, stand up for yourself. Tell them those desires and wants. My dad quoted something to me recently that resonated; he said be sweet and kind with your words as you may very well have to swallow them later. I may not have gotten the quote exactly right but I want you to get the concept. How has it worked out in the past when you just blurted out how you felt or what you wanted to others? Did they receive it? Were they immediately on the offensive? Did it take you longer to find a common ground that you could agree on? If you said yes to any, if not all of these questions, then I would strongly urge you to try a different approach.

A large part of finding that happiness that we started off talking about is harnessing the lessons you should have learned from your experiences and actually using them. What good does it do you to go through something and still be the same way after it's over? We do not go to school and not expect to be any smarter afterwards and so we should not expect to meet people and stay the same after being in each other's lives. *STITCHES #47 - If you are still the same after having been a part of someone else's life and or they being a part of yours, you may need to reevaluate your connection.* I am not saying put them out of your life but rather let us be honest with what we allow in our lives. Most people are either in your life to watch what is going on in yours (Spectators), talk about what is going on (Gossipers - either to you or about you), or to add to your life (Enhancers). The enhance category is few and far between but the other categories most of us have a plethora of. So many that we could share some with others and still have plenty. The crazy part about this is that unfortunately we are the Gossipers or Spectator in so many of our friends lives too. This is why our lives seem stagnant or routine. Did I just call you out? Yes. I find myself guilty of this as well sometimes. We see it but only point it out in extreme cases where we change the title to an Acquaintance, someone we recognize that we are only in each other's lives for a specific reason and specific time frame. I said all of that to say this, if you find yourself or your "significant Other" finds themselves not being able to maintain their full commitment, or you notice you are not and the people in your life are not adding to each other's lives then the picture of your connection needs to be refocused on the big picture. It may be time to make some changes.

Have you ever received a message from someone that was just random? I mean, the type where you do not know how to exactly respond to it other than to just pause a second. Then there are the ones like I get from time to time, via a text message at that, and you scurry to touch bases with the culprit of such news. This happen to me one day recently; I receive a message from a dear friend who, by most people's account, should be in pre-marital bliss considering they had just got engaged approximately a month or so prior. The text message said, "I don't think I want to get married".

As you could probably imagine I was in shock. Not by the news but rather the maturity of her announcement. Allow me to explain. In my line of work, I often encounter people who think they know what they want but have no idea. It is really pathetic actually. I find that equal to one who is blind but runs around pretending and claiming they are not. The sad part is everyone else clearly sees their defect and often tells them but they are not at a stage in their process to accept anything from anyone concerning their lives.

I gasp at how many single folk walk around complaining about not being married and how many married folks want to do single folk stuff. Please allow me to elaborate. A tragedy of great magnitude has occurred where people are in love with the picture of marriage but know very little and have no desire to understand the complexity or reality of it. This is the very reason why according to statistics 55% of marriages end in divorce. Look at it like this, our lives are like seasons, like new born babies we could not stay that way forever, no matter how much our parents wanted us to. The same thing can be said about singleness. If it is your time to be single, enjoy it, regardless of how long or short it last. There are pros and cons to each stage and season of lives.

If you are married, stop complaining and change your motives. For whatever reason you decided to make the commitment, stop looking for loopholes and a back door out. Whatever desires you aloud to lead you to joining in matrimony, a sense of duty should direct you now that you are there. I know some of you are reading this and saying you cannot be talking about me and I do not know your story. Well, you are absolutely right about the not knowing your story but I am talking to you. As people we make things so much more complicated than they have to be. *STITCHES # 100 - Move forward or move on, either way, just make a decision.* Things happen in relationships. You have two choices; you can either forgive and move forward with the relationship or move on. Understand that if the person has wronged you, they may or may not do it again. Depending on what it is, on purpose or not, it could happen. Can you handle it if it does and are you going to hold this experience against them?

If you cannot move forward, then move on. Move on with your life. Move on with what you feel is a better situation for you.

One of the worst things you can do to yourself and others is to know that you are not able to move past something and not tell whoever else is involved. It is not fair and it ultimately leads to a cascade of monumental disappointment. If you have ever found yourself on the bunt end of an argument and did not even understand why, then you may be a victim of a suppressed unforgiveness moment that has manifested in another arena altogether. *STITCHES # 109 - You cannot fight someone who will not get in the ring with you.* It is twice as hard to fight someone when they do not tell you that you are even in the ring fighting. Like singleness, marriage has its pros and cons too. If you married someone for what they can do for you then that is the start of your problems. Being married to someone is about what you can do for each other and it should actually be a challenge between the two of you to see who can serve the other. It is not a competition but a duty to display what the other person means to you.

I speak to this guy often who is a few years older than I, back on his first of two marriages, and he will quickly tell you he is still trying to figure things out. Before you ask, he got married, divorced his first wife, remarried, sometime later divorced her and went back to this first wife. Anyways, he often tells of how it took him being with someone else to realize what he had all along. Side note: *STITCHES # 112 - Stop trying to hold on to someone who is trying to go. It might take going for them to learn what it means to stay.* One day the gentleman asked what advice I could give for two situations. He knew that his marriage, like so many others he has talked to, just was not the same after the honeymoon phase was over. His second question was what can he do to change the atmosphere of their relationship? Let me reiterate something I said earlier that in case you did not get, you need to hear it again - RELATIONSHIPS ARE WORK!

Chapter 17

Compromise vs. Negotiating

I often joke with people when I tell them that my biggest challenge is getting the light bulb to come on for people without actually flipping the switch. We often want to just bypass the steps and flip the switch on ourselves but we really are not helping when we do this. In fact, we are probably causing more harm than good, at least for us that is. If you want your spouse to respond a certain way or do certain things and you have tried just coming out and telling them and it still has not worked or happen, then you need to deploy some tactics to create the effect you are looking for. If you do not feel your partner is satisfying your sexual appetite, have a discussion one night, preferably after sex, about you supplying and fulfilling their needs. Timing is important. If you bring up the subject when sex is not in play then you risk the wrong message going forward and then you have to do damage control. Start the discussion by asking what you can do to better please them. If they do not know, be prepared to offer ideas and suggestions. Do not go into the talk expecting them to have answers necessarily and then both of you be at a lost when they do not. The talk will not last long and nothing that you set out to talk about would have been discussed. After the discussion is on the way, negotiate a deal where you do not get everything you want but you are getting more than what you came unto the talk with. This method should be repeated. *STITCHES #113 – Marriage and relationships are not about compromise, they are about negotiations.* Many of us have been taught that relationships were all about compromise. Well let me dispel this grievous untruth. In a compromise, one person wins and the other person loses. If your entire relationship is based on one of you winning and the other losing then eventually it becomes a competition on who can win the most. When this happens, someone will always loose too much. That person is like a silent bomb waiting to explode. They will get to the point where losing will no longer be an option for them and then the relationship will completely break down. They will not want to even consider fixing things are working things out. This is why I feel relationships should be about negotiations. In a negotiation, both parties get something but neither gets everything that they may have set out for. In a negotiation, communication is the key. It is the only way both parties leave with something. It is also a sure fire way to keep the lines of communications open.

The other question was about changing the atmosphere of your relationship. This begins by changing your attitude toward the change. If you are not optimistic then change is not coming. It is irrelevant if you want things to change if all you do is talk negatively about it. You can speak life and death through your tongue. You can change the atmosphere at your job, in your vehicle, in your relationship or marriage by simply changing how you treat them. I challenged the older guy by asking when was the last time he did something out of the norm for his wife. Giving a woman your credit card and or some money and saying, "Get yourself something nice on me" does not contribute to your need. When was the last time you left a note in a place where you knew she would pass? It does not have to cost a great deal of money. Simply try putting your thoughts into your actions. People notice and your atmosphere will begin to be better.

"I am...because until you know who you are then you won't know what you are supposed to do."
Author Unknown

Although the writer of this statement is anonymous, the words regenerate in the truthfulness. Sometimes we also need to learn how to not ignore what is right in front of us. I asked a friend to ride with me to an appointment. It was my hope that we would get better acquainted and I would get a deeper understanding as to why she viewed the world in the way she does. The trip initiated with the normal pleasantries with the exception of her being late for the originally discussed departure time. It bothered me not as I expected it. As we road, we made small talk and listened to music. I turned on a mix music channel in an attempt to make her feel comfortable. I soon discovered that my attempt was feudal as she was clearly lost as we listen to songs that were not even my desired listening selections. I was attempting to find a happy medium but was clearly failing. A couple of the songs struck her familiar interest but nothing to annotate symbolism of her having a good time. The conversation was equally plain. On the way back, the radio happen to pick up a local station which immediately drew her in as nectar draws a bee. She began singing and immediately asked if I would turn it up. The striking thing about the songs that were playing on the station was one out of about twenty I had never even heard before or agreed with. After reminiscing about this experience, I realized that there were several lessons to be taken away for this experience. Everyone who we get along with does not necessarily mean they are meant to be our friends. Some people are meant to be nothing more than an acquaintance. We ignore the obvious signs that we are unequally yoked and push or should I say lean on the few, and I do mean few things that we have in common. Now I know that sentence kind of alarmed you because I used two words familiar to most, unequally yoked. You can probably hear your parents in your ears right now saying you should stay away from that boy or girl because you all were unequally yoked. Well, allow me to shed some light on this concept for you. For most this phase, equally yoked or unequally yoked, was taken from a biblical text referring to being "saved" verses "unsaved". My experience however has taught me that this phase means so much more. To me, the phase equally yoked means seeing things with the same concept; being fundamentally on the same page. Just as two people can grow up in the same house and receive the same opportunities, they can end up viewing the world very differently. Being equally yoked means fining that someone who views the world the way you view it. It does not mean you will agree on everything or on every point but you agree on agreed upon foundations that you can rely on. For example, a person who was raised by someone who found it socially acceptable to receive handouts verses someone who grew up with someone who refused to take any or allow them to receive any will fundamentally differ in their outlook of work and receiving help. This will not make either person better or worse than the other but rather it will just mean they are what I call unequally yoked on certain levels.

Everyone has desires when they start or even before they meet someone but somewhere along the line after they meet, things change. Is it that society has cultured us into looking at the negatives in life that we focus on them and do not see the cup as half full but rather half empty? Whichever the case, in order to obtain or reached the place we at least call contentment, we must get over our own hurdles or we will never face the ones of life with a legitimate chance. In order to do this we must begin to not just look at the big picture but to look at things from a big picture perspective. Most of us would agree that we try and see things from a big picture occasionally but due to the regiment of life, most of us get caught up in the view that we forget about the picture. It is like looking through a pair of binoculars. We see what we desire up close and with depth. The only drawback is that the view blocks out ninety percent of the rest of our view. Things coming from the side or even right next to us are blocked. When we remove the binoculars we can see what we have been missing but we choose, more often than not, to block out the rest of the picture just to see the view up close by the binoculars. It is not like the view is leaving or any different; we just act as if seeing it without the binoculars would take away from the appeal. The truth is some things need to be viewed and kept at a distance in our lives. By being too close to them, they prohibit us from making informed decisions. If we could treat people like they are part of the big picture of our lives and not like our life itself, then we would be better able to make informed decisions on who we allow to be both a part of our lives and who we relinquish decision making power to.

Chapter 18

When to Hold and When to Fold

When most people hear this term they immediately think of cards. Even if you have never been to a casino, you know what is meant by these two terms. Some of the most skilled players will tell you that this is one of the pentacle lessons that have to be learned in order to be successful. There are a lot of factors to consider such as how much you have invested, who you are playing against, what their history looks like, and of course, the house. We all face similar challenges when involved with someone. We must evaluate the entire picture, not just the one which is causing the most grief at that moment. We must look at how much we have put into the investment. This is where things get tricky for a lot of people. They do not realize that one of the essential keys to success in relating with other people is not what the other person is contributing but what they are. So many times we think the success or failure in the relationship rides on the shoulders of someone else but the truth is it rides on ours. You can be successful in a relationship that results in the going of separate ways by the parties involved. For instance, people invest in companies every day that they know will not result in long term gains but they will invest heavily for the short term. Our problem, like so many amateurs who play the market and lose their life's savings or retirement is we lack the wisdom of knowing how to invest what and when. Experienced Stockbrokers will tell you this comes from studying the market and having a diversified portfolio. Some people that we meet were never meant to yield long term gains but yet we invest like there is no tomorrow. So the first part of our understanding that needs to change is what we invest. The first stage needs to be learning or examining the market. Learn the treads. See what works and what does not. Ask questions from those with more experience. You can learn just as much from a loser as you can from a winner. The loser will show you all the things that did not work. A winner will teach you some of the factors that did. I say some because no two portfolios should be the same. Just copying off of someone else's work will not work in the real world just as it did not in grade school. What worked today for one person may not necessarily work tomorrow.

After examining the present market, take notes of the atmospheric changes. Certain times of year bring about certain adaptations. Your partner may be less responsive or communicative during the Christmas season then other parts of the year. By recognizing this, you can actually save yourself some heartache. I remember constantly asking my wife if she was ok. She began to tell that it worked on her last nerve. Although I was concerned and noticing changes in her behavior, I really needed to focus on the why instead of the what. Why was she acting differently and not on what or if I had did wrong. As people, we always think we have done something. Note to everyone. *STITCHES #114 Sometimes people just want to be left to their thoughts.* Give them time and space and if it is a good investment, it will yield positive dividends and those earnings will come back to you.

The next step in examining your investment after determining when to invest is determining how much to invest. This can be tricky because our human nature says go all in all the time and as fast as you can when things seem hot. I believe this could not be further from what is right. There should be even more caution and regard when things are going smoothly or hot. For instance, when you first meet someone and everything appears to be going extremely well. Most people begin to want to spend every waking moment with their new found experience. This is actually very dangerous and risky. The reason is because you do not know them. Not even a little bit. There are some lessons that are only taught over time. It is like going to math class and saying on day three, can I have the midterm so I can determine if I will pass or fail this class. I know everyone wants to decide as quickly and early as possible in a relationship if someone is wasting their time or if the compound moments are going anywhere but there are no substitutions and early testing. You must take your time and invest a little at a time. This is key. No matter how hot or popping things seems to be. No one wants to be caught with their pants down standing in front of smoke and mirrors. No one likes this feeling. What needs to happen is you need to create a plan. The plan needs to be one of gradual progression. It should not be compromised or renegotiate too many times. Otherwise you will end up throwing it out and moving forward without one; which is equally as bad. You always here fitness experts talk about needing to create a plan to get yourself into shape or back into it. A lot of people think they can cover up years of poor eating and exercise habits with a couple weeks of strict dieting. This does not work and most people who do this end up binge eating and gaining more weight afterwards then they had originally. My point is it actually takes times to get where you want to go. I struggled for years with saying I was going to get back in shape and develop the beach body I always wanted but all I did was talk about wanting to do it. I never took the necessary steps in order to make it a reality until I made serious changes in how I went about doing things. I am not where I want to be yet but I feel better than I have in too many years to count. It is started with me having a plan and sticking to it. Not just at the beginning but until I saw results.

Now I am on my way to that body and I have the drive and fortitude to get there. You have to create a plan for progression in order to move to the next level. When I go to the gym, I do not just start with the heaviest weights in there and see how many I can do; I will quickly hurt myself. Same concept applies to relationships. You have to start easily; on a level where both sides are equal. Even if you both think you can handle it, you may want to dial it back a little because you do not want to create a strain that neither of you saw coming. Any weight lifter will tell you when lifting dumbbells or bench presses; you must make sure both sides have the same amount of weight. Otherwise, it can cause a strain on your body and you can hurt yourself. Even to the extent that a muscle cannot recover. So, in determining how to invest, I suggest overwhelmingly to begin with just Talking. *STITCHES #6 - Communicate early and often.* The problem that so many people make is they fail to talk, on purpose. You probably say this is ludicrous but believe it or not, you may have yourself. Anytime you tell yourself not to say something to your partner, you are actually hindering the communication process. *STITCHES #7 - Whether it hurts or strokes communication is the largest challenge for every relationship.* When it lacks, the relationship is a ticking time bomb; just waiting to explode.

Examples of a plan for progression consist of things like, number of dates before letting him pick up the bill and not going Dutch anymore, first kiss, cuddling, public affection, meeting kids, meeting friends, meeting parents, etc. Now, I know some of you have your particulars about who pays on a date. I, myself, grew up with the rule that the woman was not paying for anything and that it was not even open for discussion. I later found out that fathers were telling their daughters to pay for their own so they would not have to feel any obligation to their date. Times have changed and women want a sense of independence. By the way, women, *STITCHES #160 - Every man wants a woman who has a sense of independency but no man wants to be with a woman who is just independent.* Otherwise, he does not feel that she needs him.

The plans for progression can be regulated by set milestones such as a set number of dates or time between dates. One of the craziest things I hear people say is if the date is good tonight, I am going to see them tomorrow. Wrong! This is how we mess up. We cause ourselves to emotionally attach before finding out enough information to make a logical decision. Emotions mess us up. Male or female, it does not matter. If he brought you roses and did not try and get a night cap the first night, it does not mean he is not a dog. Gentleman, just because she appears to have it all together juggling an eight to five job, kids, and a home life does not mean that there are not some habits that could cause major problems down the road. You can set other milestones such as types of settings you find yourself in and dinner and a movie at each other's place. Although it is nice to get out of the public eye and have some private moments, this could move things along to fast. Have dinner with each other's friends. This is another way of determining compatibility. Your friends are excellent judges of character and they know what you are like so they can test the atmosphere for unseen static energy.

At this point you have determined the investment, when and where to invest, let us take a moment to talk about the other party involved. Apart from all the other factors involved in investing, you have to take a solid look at what you are investing in. What is its worth? How forthcoming is it with its shortcomings? Too upfront is a sign just as well as acting like it does not have any at all. Everything has drawbacks and shortcomings. I like to call them side effects. I heard a female Comedian say once that she wished men came with warning labels like products do. They would help you make better decisions. Well I offer that all of us do come with labels; except they are not side effect labels but rather warning labels. There are millions of traffic signs on the roads. Some are bright red that say stop, others are yellow for caution and orange for information. Yet with all the free information, there are hundreds of accidents every day of people failing to pay attention to the warning signs and informational signals. They just blow right pass the signs as if they do not even exist. The same can be said about the people we find ourselves involved in. Everyone has that family member that no one would leave their child alone with or that co-worker that no one trusts with any personal business because quite simply, they cannot hold water. These people did not just walk up to us and tell us they have flaws, we saw their warning labels from a distance, over time. To some degree, we had to take the time to get to know them. That is my advice for your investment. Invest a little of you while you explore the investment. As you grow more interested, invest more. Never invest everything; even after you are married. You always need to keep a sense of you for yourself and your partner. You need this because it is what keeps you desiring one another and intrigued about each other's growth. I hear people say all the time that they invested so much of themselves in their relationship or marriage and then it did not work out. Folks, I'm a realist, none of us are God so none of us know that the relationship or marriage we are in is it and that there will not become a time when we will be back on the market or shopping so we all need to act accordingly. I jokingly talk to my wife like I do not know her and I am trying to pick her up from time to time. This keeps her wanting to look good for me and it keeps me wanting to still have the swagger I had to get her in the first place. We need to function as though we are making the best of right now because the next second might hinder us from doing what we planned or considered. The Creator of the universe does not consult with us when he is ready to make a decision.

Conducting a background check on your investment is highly advised. No one puts their money on something without making sure it is not a scam or poor investment. Well, not anyone who considers themselves smart that is. Some backgrounds need more than just the traditional check as well. I am not telling you to go look up folks' ex's but have conversations with the friends, family, ministers, co-workers, and anybody they are willing to expose you to. I am not saying to be all obvious with your investigation but we are talking about the greatest investment you will ever make; one that you expect compound returns of your investment from. So why would you not want to take as much time as necessary to make sure it is worth it.

Lastly, let us discuss the house. In cards, the house always gets its cut. The same goes for life. Things are going to happen. Prepare for them. It is nice to hope and dream but this is not the Wizard of Oz and we are not in a fairy tale. So prepare for the chaos that will come. Although you may not be able to prepare for every challenge, you can stay prepared for one and adjust accordingly when it arises. This is also the stage where you have to make some decisions. Periodically during investing, your portfolio needs to be reviewed to determine if there are any changes that need to be made. This is the stage that I called, knowing when to hold and when to fold. We have all been there, had that friend that we knew was no good for us or that boy that our parents warned us would break our heart but yet we did not listen and now we are picking up the pieces.

This issue also goes deeper though. Some of us have significant others or spouses that we know are not good investments. We married them thinking that if we poured more into them they would reap a greater reward but it has not panned out and now you are confused; tossed between weather to honor your heart and stop wasting your time or continue hoping for things to change because of family and religious factors. As you will hear me say often, I cannot make this decision for you and no one should make it for you. At the end of the day, you have to live with the decision. Everyone deserves happiness. It is what we all seek. We just find ourselves often in a position where we compromise and settle. The issue with settling is that you lose who you really are in the process. We all know people or we are one of those people who have settled so much that they do not even know what they want anymore. They are just going through the motions. To you I offer the advice that was once shared with me during one of my lowest points, go back to where your happiness left you and start from there to determine what caused your change and make some changes. This includes cutting people out of your life.

WHAT ABOUT IF I FOLD

Ninety-nine percent of people do not enter a relationship or marriage with the intent of planning an exit strategy or determining when it will be time to close up shop and move on. Yet, millions of people do it every day. The people are all different and although scenarios have their commonalities, no two situations are the same. They are all filled with their complexities and individuality. But what separates them? How do you answer the age old question of whether it is worth it to stick it out or to simple count your losses?

This question has plagued relationships since the beginning of time. When is enough, enough?
 If you want to test your part, just place your relationship on the seesaw scale. I call it the seesaw scale. I call it the seesaw scale because you can view your contributions to the relationship the same as you would if you and your partner were on a seesaw together. You do not really realize that you are doing so much work until you notice the other person. They have not been putting in work but rather just going through the motions. To

check their contributions, stop pushing off. Things will still continue to go up and down for a minute due to gravity. They will complain because they will see the difference. They may even attempt to make you feel guilty about doing what it seems like you have always done. This is but a ploy to get you grinding again. At some point the seesaw will stop and the two of you will be level. It is at this point that you will realize just how much the other person was using you.

This analogy appeared to be about playing on a seesaw but it is really how we should treat the people we choose to relate to. They may appear to have it together and care deeply for you but if they are not holding up their end of the deal, then sooner or later it will go south. This is when you will know you have to fold. It is that moment when you realize that you are the only one playing in a two person sport. When you see that they have left you with all the cards. Regardless of whether everyone is staring or not, you must do what is best for you at this movement.

Folding is not easy. It can be done in one or two ways. You can choose to address it in an adult manner or as a child. The problem with most people is not that they cannot see problems but they handle them poorly. I heard myself quoting a comedian recently by saying "I'm a grown A man". It is funny but true. Being grown comes with a stigma. You need to handle things differently than how you did as a child. If your partner is not treating you the way you deserve or expect, go to them; communicate to them in a non-judgmental or threatening way that there is a situation. Let them know it is a situation that has the potential to turn into a problem if not addressed. DO NOT NAG!! This goes for males or females. Nobody wants anybody who is hanging on their shirt tail like a spoiled two year old. State your case, give opportunity for the issues to be addressed, communicate clearly the possible repercussions, and be prepared to act on your standards if they are not met.

Chapter 19

Change is Reflective

Most people claim change; they either want it, recognize it or try to avoid it. The truth is the very thing that drives most things in life is the existence of change. I was speaking with someone who told me repeatedly that they were battling with what seem to be an inward struggle. They described it as unto two powerful forces at odds with each other. They believed their subconscious was confused. After spending some time listening to their story, it was clear that they were indeed facing an inner battle. Their beliefs, experiences, desires, and hopes were all singing different tunes. When they were young, they were grounded and rooted on their beliefs. It served as a launching pad for their dreams. They were taught to believe the sky was the limit and there was no extent to where the sky stopped. Their desires were attached to their beliefs and created visions of what could and may be. In some circumstances, experiences enhanced these beliefs and desires but in many it only hindered them. Although, the sky is big and covers the air as far as you can see, unfortunately it is not until you start the journey to reach the sky that you find it takes much more work than originally thought or believed.

Not too long ago, I was having a discussion with my wife about expectations that I had which I was mildly disappointed were not being fulfilled. I continued to press the issue before she responded, "What about the expectations that I had or have?" After some thought about what she had said, I realized she was right. All too often we point out how others, especially our Significant others, fall short of our expectation but either "blow off" or overlook when we fall short ourselves. As you get older, you learn to choose your battles wisely and to know when to pack up your gear and wait to fight another day. I chose to step back and do what all men do when they realize their woman is somewhat right, I shut up and internalized the conversation.

We all talk about how horrible our conditions are from time to time, but few of us are willing and ready to do what is necessary to bring about true change. Folks, I am about to save you a world of hurt, misery, and frustration if you can just digest this next statement, *STITCHES #94 Change is reflective but it begins with you.* If you want someone to change, change yourself. We spend countless hours talking about how people are and how they act but as my mom use to always tell me, "you have to figure out who you dealing with and what you are dealing with because then and only then you will know how to deal with them". If you want someone to change, start making small but noticeable changes about yourself. If your spouse does not expect you to take her car and fill it up with gas then do it. Try running your husband's bath water or having his favorite dish prepared and ready when he arrives home. Use a little more care and attention. You may be surprised at how much more cooperative the other person or people are when they see the change in you.

Recently, I asked someone if two wrongs make a right and they replied yes. Now, let me pause here and say I understand that the majority of those of you reading this disagree with the response to this question being yes. The other half are applauding and do not know where to begin to fathom how this answer could be anything but no. You would even go so far as to say that this response should go without saying. The truth in all of this is that there is no right or wrong answer.

Chapter 20

Moving Forward

There comes a time in all our lives when the sun does not shine the way it once did. The flowers do not seem to desire to bloom anymore and nothing in the world seem right. Food does not taste the same and the moments that use to take your breath away are but such a memory you often wonder if they even really happen or were they a dream. No one looks to close chapters in their lives but they are necessary in order for the next one to begin. With this in mine, we must discuss the concept of moving forward.

First and foremost, understand that moving forward is not a means to an end but a transition to the next season of experiences. Too often we see changes in our lives, especially those that we felt would last forever as cliff hangers or book finishers instead of what they really were, mere chapter closers. I was advising a woman once whose name we will call Jane. She had been separated from her husband for several months. Prior to the separation, she suffered what most would consider a series of catastrophic events in her life. She lost her best friend and two other close relatives all within about a year and a half. She was totally distorted. She lost her sense of connection with her husband, kids, work, and everything around her. She was not eating and refused medical assistance for some time. The experience drove her husband to a seclusion of his own. After months of counseling, she began to work her way back to a state of normalcy but possibly too late. Her husband decided to take a job in their home town and because obligations of her own with her job, she was forced to allow her kids and husband to move away. She visited when she could but it never seemed to be enough. The husband finally asked for a divorce. She exhausted numerous pleas of begging, request to go through counseling, and anything else she could think of but nothing seem to move him.

Before you jump to conclusions and call him less than a man, let us look at his side of the story. Mark, as we will call him, had known Jane for years and had always been her biggest fan. When she experienced her lost, he cried and comforted her. Her refusal to move forward and get back to a state of normalcy eventually became too much. He pleaded with her to do simple task like feeding and bathing the kids, picking up the kids from school, and helping out with his job when times were busy and he could really use the extra help. To no avail, Jane remained secluded and emotionless. He begged her to go to counseling but she would always come with a new excuse. He grew tired of his needs and concerns of their children not being addressed that when the opportunity came to move home where he would get the support he felt they so desperately desired, he moved.

Mark came to a very rash conclusion; there is a slim line between waiting on someone to come along and prolonging the inevitable. Although he loved his wife, he had to look at the facts and the potential of the situation. We cannot stand by idly and tell ourselves that our situation is getting better and it is not. *STITCHES # 184 - there is a difference between not doing anything and not doing nothing.* You cannot stand by idling and not doing anything to solve your problems. Stop expecting the answers to just fall from the sky. Like the old saying goes, anything worth having is worth working for; anything that changes needs something to happen in order for it to occur. Too often we hide behind the mirrors of life expecting things to change as you watch it from a spectator's seat. Please know that life will pass you by with this attitude. If you want to make more money, take your butt to school or back to it and learn something that will help you make more. You want to improve your relationships, put yourself in the position to make things better for you and your life. Change your work habits if you want to be noticed. Stop complaining about how the boss always points out your flaws and praises others. Be grateful that they do notice you and work on those areas while simultaneously sustaining your attributes. If you want your relationship to change, evaluate it for what it is and adjust accordingly. You do not need anyone to tell you if your partner is worth your time or if they value you. I asked someone once what the difference was in waiting on someone to change and prolonging the inevitable. I got all kinds of the same safe answers but the truth is the answer lies in the beholder. Stop looking for someone to tell you to move on or stick it out. Although advice is nice, ultimately you are the one in the position and wearing the shoes, so act like it and walk out whatever decision you are going to make. And guess what, if you make a decision and do not like the way things are going as you start down the road with it, change directions. The key is to keep moving forward. If you are not moving forward than anything else is a step in the wrong direction.

Often the hardest thing to admit and see is what is right in front of us. Maybe it is because we are too close or maybe it is because we just do not want to see some things. Whatever the reason, too often we find ourselves on the wrong side of a situation only because we are looking at it wrong. Today, I found myself telling two totally different people dealing with two totally different issues, the same advice, *STITCHES #180 - the answers to your issue is in your perspective.*

Scenario #1 - A kid was complaining about his teacher and how he felt he was unjustly being treated. He complained of how he deserved respect and that the teacher did not understand him or have a right to treat him the way she was. The problem with this incident is that it is all too common. I went on to explain to the student that life will not always deal you a fair hand. Just like in cards, you can either complain or just hold your cards but in this case, your situation will never get better. The other option is you can trade your cards in. There is a risk with this method also. Sometimes, you will get better cards and sometimes you get worse. Just like life, there are no guarantees that you will be dealt a better hand, you just have to know that a different hand is different than the one you have. I further explained to the young man, just as much as it is about what you think, it is all about how you see it. I pointed out a plant which seemed to not be too far from where he sat. After asking him to look at it for a moment, I asked him to get up and move to another spot in the room and then look at the same plant again. I asked him to describe what he saw and one of the first things he mentioned was how the difference in positions changed his perspective and vanish point. He saw sunlight from the new position where he had not before. *STITCH #132 - If you want to see your world differently quit complaining about the circumstances and change your position.*

Chapter 21

Change in Perspective

I woke up one morning with the thought, "Let's change the world today". The strange part about this statement was not that I was getting up that morning after having come up with this elaborate plan in my sleep to find a cure for cancer or how to solve the equation to bring about world peace but simply that I was going to the gym to perform my daily workout. This was not even out the ordinary this day because I had woken up many days prior with the same plan to work out before I began my day. What made this day different was my drive; my passion. It is not so much about me anymore but of me. When I change things in me then my immediate world is affected and thus, it changes. You have to know that when your world changes, the rest of the world has no choice but to follow suit. I remember hearing my wife harp repeatedly talking about the weight she had gained, how much she wants or needs to loose and like so many people, this is where the buck stops. They only talk about the changes they want to see. At some point you have to push yourself past the want and create a desire and passion. Desire is you seeing yourself where you want to be or having a vision and passion is the deep desire to pursue that vision until it becomes a reality; whether this is your physical appearance, your emotional stability, or relational status.

OUR CONTRIBUTION TO THE WORLD

Let's face it, very few people are born with a silver spoon in their mouth. And even those people have the same problems that the rest of us do; it is just under a different set of conditions. In life we are dealt a hand, it is not always the best one or the one we would choose if it were our choice. Nevertheless, it is what it is and it was not our choice to whom, when, and where we were born. There were other powers that we have no control over, at work. Knowing this is actually a step up instead of a setback. There is always power in the hand you are dealt. It is just on you to figure out how to harness that power. Power is just like water. Let us say you are given some water, there are many different things you can do with it. You can drink it, bath in it, water plants or animals with it, swim in it, or even give it away. The power does not lie in the water itself but in how you choose to use that power. So often we focus on the negativity of things given or not given to us that we miss the very power that we have. The crazy thing about power, as in our illustration of water, is that we also have the option of simply doing nothing at all with it. So many people are scared or intimidated about making the wrong choice that they go through life failing to make choices all together. Life is not fair. Stop looking for it to be. You are not going to get away with what you see others do and sometimes get away with. Get over it already! Stop whining and complaining about your life and do something with yourself. The time you are wasting doing these things is causing your dreams, destiny and purpose that much longer to manifest.

HARNESS THE POWER IN THE HAND DEALT TO YOU

No one wakes up at the start of their day and says to themselves, "I want to get in a life threatening event today." In the same manner no one gets into an automobile with thoughts of an accident. Just think about it, you wake up to personal hygiene or beauty care, then you move on to preparing the rest of you, never pausing to think if the outfit you are wearing is your last. Millions of people go through this similar routine and then move forward to riding in their chosen mode of transportation. Then out of nowhere, their lives are sometimes temporarily postponed, haunted, or terminated. Despite the options of total annihilation looming, people get up and risk it every day. This is the fate of us all but there are some exceptions to this state of normalcy. The exceptions are those who do what is necessary to prepare for moments such as those. Although we have but very little control over some events which occur in our lives, often we can soften the blows or prevent them simply by listening to ourselves and planning ahead. I would guesstimate that only a small percentage of the world's population are like me and think about what they are going to wear the night before while lying in their beds. An even smaller percentage of people plan pass the next day. Preparation is the essential.

It has often been said that the start of getting to the root of any problem is admitting to there being one. I know many of you are saying to yourself as you have read this, "What does this guy know about relationships?" "What makes him such a guru?" Well, allow me to reiterate that I am no guru. When asked I do not even claim to be a coach but rather an advisor. For when most of us think of coaches we think of sports. In sports, a coach may ask you do WXY in order to get Z. Well when you do WXY and do not get Z, then you look at the coach as if there was something wrong with what he told you. I believe I can only advise you as to the options you may or may not have seen. At the end of the day, the choice continues to be yours. I do not know it all nor do I claim to be an expert. I am not even close. There is no magic pill or potion which I will be selling on an infomercial in between your favorite sitcom. I can only vouch for knowing this one thing and I will let you and everyone else who likes to give people titles, determine what to call me. What is that one thing you say, I only claim to know this; you have the answers at your disposal in some way form or fashion. You have the solutions for yourself. You just sometimes need someone to guide you in the direction, to show you how to access the information you need to solve your situation. It is like having a research project in which you need to conduct some research. Although, the internet may claim to have all the answers you need and search engines like Google can almost pull up any piece of information you ask it to. If you do not know where to begin to look, then you will not know what to tell that search engine to look for. It is for this reason why I believe libraries will never become extinct. There is nothing like being able to go to a library and just start describing what you are doing or trying to accomplish and dealing with a live person who seemingly picks up where your road ends on your dead end street and they direct you to other options. This is the same thing which millions of people do when they go and see a professional. That professional is not trained to know all the answers but rather to help people locate their own answers. Now, do not get me wrong, this is a very challenging and tedious task. It is this same concept that I believe this book is all about. Taking what you know and directing it in the right structure for formidable results.

So you have been reading this book and probably nodding your head and even high lighting a few good points (hint, hint, hint), as you should, but do you really get it? And if so, what is it that you get exactly? Well allow me to break this down for you because I want to make sure you got it and when you go to share (another hint), I want to ensure you really help them.

It is simply not enough to talk about change if you do not recognize it. Change is growth. If you do not grow than you are dying. I love my wife but at one point I grew tired, like so many others do, of the same day in and day out retinue or rhetoric. She was doing her thing and so was I. We simply stop growing together. It was not that we stop loving each other or that we did not want to be together anymore. We just stop growing together and our change started going the opposite way of each other. We took the time to address the head on and continue to apply the lessons we have learned. If issues go on unaddressed, a relationship is doomed; it just does not know it yet. You have to recognize the warning signs in your life when they appear. Otherwise, events in your life will leave you gasping and wondering why. Truth be told, half of the things we complain about regarding events that happen in our life did not just come out of the blue but gradually grew larger and tried to get our attention even before it climaxed. The problem is we see the warning signs and just ignore them. Particularly because we do not want to face the truth and the other is because we would rather not deal with it. We walk around acting as though if we choose to not address an issue it will go away or solve itself. Well here is my last public service announcement...... THAT WON'T HAPPEN! Leaving an issue unaddressed will no more solve the issue than acting like it does not exist.

Once you are ready to face the previously mentioned truths, then you are ready to start applying TLC (tender, love, and care) to your situation. You must be tender in how you address the issue. The matters of the heart or how a person carries them are always touchy subjects and should be approached with extreme caution. You must handle the situation in a spirit of love. Do not expect the problem to be solved overnight or according to other people's timeline. Love is patient; love is kind. And then, you have to actually care. People can tell if you are just being nice. No one likes to be patronized. If you are going to go through the motions, give them your all. Not just your best effort. These are two different things. An effort could be once and then you are ready to move on to the next big idea but when one is giving their all, they do not keep count. You may not remember how you got the wound, but if the stitches did their job then your life will not be hindered as you move forward in your life.

Bibliography

New International Version (NIV) Romans 8:28; 1 Corithans 13:4
Holy Bible, New International Version®, NIV® Copyright © 1973, 1978, 1984, 2011 by Biblica, Inc.

Timothy J. Dailey, Ph.D., is senior fellow in the Center for Marriage and Family Studies at the Family Research Council. Dr. Dailey and Peter Sprigg recently co-authored Getting It Straight: What the Research Says About Homosexuality.

1. Adrian Brune, "City Gays Skip Long-term Relationships: Study Says," Washington Blade (February 27, 04): 12.
Http://www.frc.org/get.cfm?i=IS04C02#edn5

A. P. Bell and M. S. Weinberg, Homosexualities: A Study of Diversity Among Men and Women (New York: Simon and Schuster, 1978), pp. 308, 309; See also A. P. Bell, M. S. Weinberg, and S. K. Hammersmith, Sexual Preference (Bloomington: Indiana University Press, 1981).

Paul Van de Ven et al., "A Comparative Demographic and Sexual Profile of Older Homosexually Active Men," Journal of Sex Research 34 (1997): 354.

"Sex Survey Results," Genre (October 1996), quoted in "Survey Finds 40 percent of Gay Men Have Had More Than 40 Sex Partners," Lambda Report, January 1998: 20.